Utopianism in New Age Sci-Fi

Oscar Gray

Table of Contents

Introduction

The Explanation

When people first hear that I am researching Christ figures in pop culture, they immediately start naming off various film/literature characters, such as Harry Potter, Gandalf, Superman, Neo and even ET, who fill that role.[1] All of these are familiar, recognizable figures who, as traditional Christ figures, serve as moral guides, sacrifice themselves for the greater good of humanity in some fashion and are resurrected. Their status as Christ figures is also present through imagery, as most assume a crucifixion pose at some point during their death/moment of sacrifice (even ET who dies after stretching his arms out to reach for Elliot).

This imagery of Christ is even more apparent in the most recent film incarnation of Superman, *Man of Steel*. Aside from the crucifixion pose, which is assumed by both Superman and Clark Kent on several occasions, there is a scene where the image of Christ and Kent overlap. Kent is speaking with a priest inside a church. The dialogue itself points to sacrifice, but more blatantly Kent is sitting in front of a stained glass window that depicts Christ in the Garden of Gethsemane. Throughout the scene, the camera slowly pans around Kent until his face replaces the image of Christ in the window and the illuminated halo in the window shines around Kent's head. His transformation into Christ is complete.

After having this discussion with the well-meaning souls who ask what my dissertation is about and, in essence, "geeking out" with them over various moments in film, I have to explain that these are not the Christ figures that I am looking for; I want to move

---

[1] The tone of this introduction is purposefully casual. A majority of the critics I have read for this dissertation – such as Stephen Prothero, Victoria Nelson, and Rhonda Wilcox, to name a few – have reflected this same casualness in the setup of their arguments. I decided to emulate their style because I believe this is the trend that cultural and pop cultural criticism is following.

away from film and literature. This usually leads to a discussion of television shows with strong Christ figures, such as *Smallville* or maybe even *Joan of Arcadia*. More likely, the conversation will include *Doctor Who* – a character who saves the world over and over again and has the ability to "die" and resurrect/regenerate actually built into his backstory. He has a personal interest in Earth, being the only one of his people (the Time Lords) left in existence. He is a warrior and a savior for humanity who loves humans even though they fail repeatedly, and continues working to save them because he hopes they will eventually get better, transcend. And he is not alone. A spinoff of the *Doctor Who* universe is *Torchwood*, a show that takes its title from an anagram of its predecessor. In *Torchwood*, the lead character, Captain Jack Harkness, dies saving humanity but is resurrected in a time vortex and is now immortal (which is a greatly simplified version of events). He can be killed, but within a few moments, he comes back to life. He and his team work to protect the world from various threats. Jack even gives up his life force to stop the shadow of death emanating from an apocalyptic demon/angel, Abaddon, and is dead for three days and nights before resurrecting on the fourth day. These are definitely Christ figures on television, but still not what I am looking for.

I am examining modern day Christ figures in American-produced fringe/cult television shows – specifically *The X-Files*, *Supernatural*, and *Buffy, the Vampire Slayer* (*Buffy*) – who, while actively working to save the world/humanity, are doing it without any expectation of a heavenly reward or even a change in the status quo of society.[2] These

---

[2] By this I mean shows not normally considered mainstream dramas or comedies. The fringe genres usually include, but are not limited to, fantasy or science-fiction based stories. "Cult" television generally means programs that have a (sometimes small) passionate, (sometimes rabid), highly devoted fan-base. For a more in-depth clarification, see Matt Hills' "Defining Cult TV: Texts, Inter-Texts and Fan Audiences" (2004) as published in *The Television Studies Reader* (eds Robert Clyde Allen and Annette Hill).

modern Christ figures, or Common Christs as I call them, are people who are less likely to be the image of sinless perfection and, more often, violent and profane saviors who do not always repent of their sinful ways. They fit Umberto Eco's description of a "real hero" by being reluctant heroes; "they die, but they would rather not die," Eco says, claiming that they would choose not to be sacrificial heroes if they could (*Travels in Hyperreality* 122).[3] These recent stand-ins are usually from blue-collar or lower class backgrounds; they are the Christs of the common man, or as Gregory Sakal describes them in "No Big Win: Themes of Sacrifice, Salvation and Redemption," they are "plain folk, pulled from the fabric of 'normal life,' and thrown into the eternal struggle between good and evil" (240). Generally, these Common Christs are in opposition with the dogmatic authority of the Christian church. The storylines that have Common Christs as their heroes often depict the organized religion of the church as an enemy, a negative influence trying to prevent the salvation of the common man by the common man.

The purpose of my dissertation is to examine Common Christs as they appear in cult television shows that embrace and make strong use of Christian mythology without being considered Christian television. I hope, through this examination, to open a conversation about how pop culture reflects the changing face of Christianity in America and whether or not it can envision future changes.

---

[3] Eco also describes a "real hero" as always being "a hero by mistake; he dreams of being an honest coward like everybody else" (122). For the figures I am working with, "mistake" is not quite the correct word. Sam and Dean Winchester, for instance, are thrust into heroic circumstances through divine fate/intervention. Likewise, Buffy Summers is "the chosen one," fated to be a vampire slayer. All three are reluctant heroes who have moments of rebellion when they try NOT to be the hero, to live "normally." There are episodes in both *Buffy* and *Supernatural* where the protagonists explore what life would be like if they were not heroes. "Mistake" implies a random chance, and that does not necessarily apply here.

Putting a Camel through the Eye of a Needle

There are reasons for being so specific, one of which is the vast number of portrayals

of Christ/Christ figures and Christianity in American film and literature. According to

Stephen Prothero's *God is Not One*, there are more books about Jesus than any other

historical figure (about seventeen thousand) currently held in the Library of Congress in

Washington, DC, with an estimated 187,000 books about Jesus in five hundred different

languages being tallied worldwide (70-71). While it is true that not all of these would be

fictional representations of Christ, the number of possibilities is still incredibly high. To try

and discuss all literary Christ figures, traditional and contemporary, is beyond the scope of

my current project.

Of course, the same complaint of vastness could be applied to Christ figures in

television shows – even in the cult/fringe genre I am focusing on – which is why I have

limited my discussion to *Supernatural, Buffy,* and *The X-Files*. The same process of

limitation could easily be applied to literature. There are, after all, any number of classic,

canonical Christ figures, such as Jim Conklin in Stephen Crane's *The Red Badge of Courage*

(1895); the eponymous characters of Harriet Beecher Stowe's *Uncle Tom's Cabin* (1852) or

Herman Melville's *Billy Budd* (1891, 1924); Jim Casey or Tom Joad in John Steinbeck's *The*

Grapes of Wrath (1939). I could even take a few canonical Christ figures and compare them

to Christ figures of more contemporary literature, such as Finny from John Knowles' *A*

Separate Peace (1959); Simon from William Golding's *Lord of the Flies* (1954); John

Coffey from Stephen King's *The Green Mile* (1996); or countless others.

One could even make the same move of separating out the pulp or popular fiction

genre and look at Christ figures such as Aslan from C.S. Lewis' *The Chronicles of Narnia:*

The Lion, the Witch and the Wardrobe (1950), Frodo in J.R.R. Tolkien's *Lord of the Rings*

(1954) trilogy, Harry Potter from the wildly popular series by J. K. Rowling (1998-2008), or

Katniss Everdeen and Peeta Mellark from Suzanne Collins' *Hunger Games* (2008-2010)

series, just to name a few. The point is, there is no shortage of literary Christ or Common

Christ figures to be examined. There would be little to no difficulty separating out a few

Christ figures and tracing their evolution within these works, and I do see elements of the

Common Christs I am identifying in these popular texts. With the exception of Aslan – who

sacrifices himself with the full knowledge that he will be resurrected – all the other Christ

figures from these popular titles are thrust into a circumstance or destiny without knowing

whether they will survive or succeed. They are Eco's "reluctant hero" and Sakal's "plain

folk"; they each enter into the larger battle not out of personal want or desire, but as an act of

protecting family or friends. They expect a changed outcome of the world, but not "heaven

on earth."

These characters are basically accepted as canonical Christ figures by the majority of

critics, so much so that the discussion moves away from looking at the actual Christ figure

within the work. Within about thirty years after the publication of *The Grapes of Wrath*, for

example, most critics were focusing less on who or what the Christ figure in the text was or

what it meant to American culture, and more on either the religious or political rhetoric

surrounding it, as in Charles T. Dougherty's "The Christ-Figure in *The Grapes of Wrath*"

(1962). The same thing happens in Tamara Rombold's "Biblical Inversion in *The Grapes of

Wrath*" (1987). In his 2005 article, "Jesus as a Cultural Hero: Steinbeck's Use of the Christ

Figure in *The Grapes of Wrath*," John J. Han cites over a dozen Steinbeck scholars who have

written on his topic within the first few pages. There is no shortage of criticism about these traditional Christ figures. Even the popular fiction works have already reached the point where the Christ figure is almost a given or a secondary character. More attention has been paid to the Christ figure in some of them because of the added element of magic or, as some have called it, paganism, in works like the *Harry Potter* series or *The Chronicles of Narnia* and *Lord of the Rings*.

Popular and religious opinion varies, however, over whether any of the characters in *Harry Potter* or *The Hunger Games* can be considered Christ-like because of the elements of magic and child-on-child violence, making their inclusion in a work about Common Christ figures even harder because one would first need to validate the choice of calling them Christ-like. Derek Murphy's light-hearted yet insightful book, *Jesus Potter Harry Christ* (2011) highlights the ways in which Harry is a Christ figure but also examines why staunch religious critics are so against this comparison. J. Killinger's *God, the Devil and Harry Potter: A Christian Minister's Defense of the Beloved Novels* (2004) does something similar, though his work does not come across quite as irreverently playful as Murphy's take.

When critics do accept these characters as Christ figures, the focus turns to how the work functions religiously or politically rather than the Christ figure itself, as in Julie Clawson's *The Hunger Games and the Gospel: Bread, Circuses and the Kingdom of God* (2012) or Susan Tan's "Burn with Us: Sacrificing Childhood in *The Hunger Games*" (2013). So while there is room to hold my discussion – the evolution of the Christ figure towards a human, fallible, Common Christ – within these works, it would read a bit like mulling over the same arguments.

This feeling of repetition segues into the second reason I am drawn to Christ figures on television as opposed to in literature: influence and cultural viability. It seems odd to say that literature lacks influence, especially considering that we have spent the last several pages discussing literature, but in terms of contemporary impact, it is true. According to the World Culture Score's "Media Habits" index, the United States is 10th below the global average in reading with an average of 5.7 hours per week. In television watching, however, the United States is ranked sixth with 19 hours per week ("NOP World Culture Score").

In his book *Pop Culture Wars: Religion & the Role of Entertainment in American Life*, William D. Romanowski identifies the cultural hierarchy of high and low established by Lawrence Levine's *Highbrow/Lowbrow* (1988), with "high culture" consisting of the traditional arts: visual arts, poetry, drama, and fiction, whereas "low culture" is what we recognize as contemporary entertainment, such as movies, pop music, pulp fiction, and television (20). While Romanowski admits that these categories are fluid and arbitrary, shifting as needed to fit the cultural norms of the time, it still pans out that we usually think of high culture as the one holding the most influence in our educational pursuits, cultural ideals, and personal beliefs. It's what we are exposed to in school and what is referenced as the backdrop of social consciousness. And yet, the "low culture" of popular entertainment has gradually grown to replace it as youth cultures have gained more and more autonomy over the decades through the advent of technological advances and educational innovations. "Contemporary entertainment," claims Romanowski, "has become an important source of guidance and nurture in a society where other social institutions no longer shape the youth culture as powerfully as they once did" (215). "Low culture," it would seem, is riding high.

The growth of the literary canon reflects this as it broadens to accept authors and works that were previously deemed unworthy of acceptance or instruction, including those of pop culture texts. Universities have taken to offering courses that focus on such popular franchises/titles as *Star Trek*, *Lord of the Rings* (or just Tolkien himself), and even *Buffy*,

alongside their traditional courses on Chaucer, Shakespeare, Melville and Whitman, with

over fifty universities offering a degree in Popular Culture or Cultural Studies or maintaining

a specific Pop Culture Department.[4] As Romanowski explains, these pop culture texts

"represent, both symbolically and practically, new ideas and perspectives, as well as the

culture of marginal and less powerful groups whose artistic voice is the contemporary media

and popular culture" (305). As such, the works of pop culture have themselves become a

social institution that offers both entertainment and leisure while still working to exert the

influence of art upon us.

But why not include film (or focus solely on film as there are enough celluloid Christ

figures to contend with) in my argument? I am looking solely at television for various

reasons, the first being a difference of audience impact between film and television. Though

a film may create a cult following (*Rocky Horror Picture Show* or *Star Wars*, for example),

there is a limited depiction for fans to interact with; the concept will not develop or evolve

beyond what was originally produced. The interpretation of the film may change, but the

original product will be the same. Robert Kolker in *Film, Form and Culture* explains that

film "delivers large emotions in intense bursts," but television programming "reflects and

refracts small, lingering, persistent, even obsessive concerns" (217). Television programs

generally run in 30 minute to one hour long episodes, at least once a week, getting between

13 and 22 episodes a season. Even if the show only runs for one season, that means it may

---

[4] The study of popular culture in a university setting began with Dr. Ray B. Browne at Bowling Green State University (BGSU) when he founded the Department of Popular Culture in 1972. Browne is also the founding editor of *Journal of Popular Culture* and *Journal of American Culture*, as well as starting the Library of Popular Culture Studies at BGSU and founding the Popular Culture Association and the American Culture Association.

have upwards of 22 hours, spread out over a period of months, to solidify its message, versus the usual one-time viewing of an hour and a half to two hours most movies receive.

Secondly, I consider the reach of television to be far greater than film. Though films may have nation or even world-wide distribution, their impact is not as immediate as television. As of 1990, the average American was reported to spend about 15% of his life watching television (Speck and Roy 1200). More recent Nielsen ratings from 2012 have clarified that amount, noting that Americans watch at least 34 hours of television a week. Even that number is not entirely correct, because surveys and ratings have a hard time accounting for all the programs that are watched on DVR/recording systems or the people who watch television programming via streaming network websites, or companies like Hulu and Netflix that are now available. There were over 300 million television sets in American households as of 2012, a number almost equal to the entire American population at that time.

Television programming has become the means by which the "normal" American judges reality and how they should respond to given situations. This alteration of perceived reality is discussed in the formation of cultivation theory, which measures the effect of television programming and advertising on "the viewer's perceived reality" as it is shaped by "heavy exposure to media and cultural imagery" (Speck and Roy 1201). In their article, "The Interrelationships Between Television Viewing, Values and Perceived Well-Being: A Global Perspective," Sandra K. Smith Speck and Ahijit Roy claim that it is through television that the "socialization of most people into standardized roles and behaviors" occurs (1201). Its main function, then, is "acculturation" (1201).

There is also a difference in reception and expectations between films and television, as well as a different impact because of the space of viewing. We go out to see movies (generally), but we stay in to watch television. It is an innocuous presence in our lives that we invite into our homes, into even the most intimate areas of our home, including the bedrooms or, in some homes, even the bathrooms. Television is a part of personal life now. It reaches out into places where other media sometimes cannot or are not accepted. As an institution, television does not require literacy or class to enjoy, and thanks to technological developments lowering the cost, it does not even require that much money to own a TV set, meaning that almost anyone can easily have access to the programming. A television signal can be found in big cities and small towns, urban centers and rural suburbs, and even in the most remote physical locations. We take no notice of seeing a television set in a business lobby or in a bar; it is accepted that most people will have at least one (usually more) in their homes. Certain refrigerators are even built with mini-television screens in the doors so that they can receive channels. This slow foray of the television set into the various areas of American life has made its programming both private and communal (Kolker 216). It is something that can be enjoyed in the privacy of one's own home or in a group, either in a domestic or commercial space. Regardless of whether a program is watched alone or with others, however, the influence of television will almost always be communal. It is a shared experience that may trigger conversations and discussions of the program, either over dinner between friends or over the Internet between thousands of fans. Since we feel secure in our surroundings and in the freedom of choice over what we watch, and with the knowledge that we are watching something "with others," we are more open and susceptible to the images presented to us.

Why *The X-Files, Buffy, the Vampire Slayer*, and *Supernatural*?

Cult and fringe television programs often allow for a different interaction of theme and character with audiences than most mainstream productions, making them a strong candidate for discussing how pop culture reflects and is informed by social belief. Programs like *The X-Files, Buffy*, and *Supernatural* do not come under the same scrutiny as mainstream network productions because of their position on the edge of culture. They are seen as quirky or "out there," and so they serve as a well-suited vehicle for examining social issues and belief systems without drawing attention to those issues. People expect socially relevant themes from mainstream dramas like *Law and Order* or *NCIS*. Some viewers are drawn to those shows for that specific reason. Fringe/cult television shows, however, with their aliens/monsters/demons and fantastical plot devices are simply considered "entertainment," so people are more willing to watch them and take in what is presented. They do not necessarily go to these shows for social instruction or commentary, but they receive it as part of the discussion/plot line.

Science fiction (on television, especially) has long been a safe textual space for the exploration of racial or sexual boundaries. Just consider *Star Trek*: the original series not only had the first interracial kiss in the episode "Plato's Step-Children" (1968), but was also one of the first shows to include various races and sexual identities in positions of power and influence in their multi-racial crew, including African American actress Nichelle Nichols as communications officer Lieutenant Nyota Uhura and gay-rights activist George Takei as helmsman Lieutenant Hikaru Sulu.[5] Later incarnations, such as *Star Trek: The Next Generation*, included examinations of sexuality and sexual inequality with the episode, "The

---

[5] Though Takei did not officially come out as homosexual until 2005, his sexual preference was something of an open secret amongst cast, crew and fans of *Star Trek* since the 1970s.

Outcast" (1992), in which the crew meet an alien race that views the expression of any sort of gender or sexual desire as a form of perversion. Similar to the social response experienced by those who came out as homosexuals in the late 1980s and early 1990s, those who exhibit gender in this world are ridiculed, outcast or forced to undergo "psychotectic therapy" to restore them to the happiness of androgyny.

The point of allowing my inner geek out to rampage unsupervised for the last paragraph is to give readers a taste of just how easy it is to find examples of storylines dealing with social issues in these types of productions. That is not to say that mainstream dramas do not have stories of social relevance or, for my purposes, moments of Christ-like sacrifice, because they do. What differentiates cult and fringe programming from the mainstream is that cult shows do not set those moments aside. In most mainstream shows, such moments or discussions would be isolated in specific arcs or billed as "a very special episode of [insert chosen TV series title here]," which gives audiences the chance to prepare themselves for it. Cult programs often just have the opportunity for these moments built into their characters/plot lines, so there is no special attention drawn to them, which allows audiences to approach the material differently. If an audience is told there is a poignant social message coming, they experience one of three responses: they pay closer attention, they overanalyze the message or the way it is presented, or they simply do not tune in because they do not want to be "preached" to. Because cult programs display these moments or characters without fanfare, audiences do not necessarily have the chance to prepare an acceptance/response. They accept it as part of the show's canon and the social commentary becomes less of a talking point and more of a discussion of how it functions in society.

This is part of the beauty of fringe/cult shows like *The X-Files*, *Buffy*, or *Supernatural*. They all rely on outlandish, non-realistic settings and circumstances, and yet they carry with them a sense of reality that causes the audience to become invested in the future of the characters. Kolker identifies this as a form of melodrama, a form that "creates empathy and identification" while also "provoking emotions, perhaps more intense than what are called for by the story being told" (172). Melodrama, according to Kolker, creates a threat that not only applies to the characters but also to the audience. It demands the audience to feel and empathize with the situation and the characters, thereby making the characters more important than the circumstances of the storyline. It is these melodramatic emotions that often demand sacrificial acts from characters for one another (Kolker 180). *The X-Files*, *Buffy*, and *Supernatural* all possess melodramatic threats and storylines and highly emotional character bonds which lead to frequent moments of self-sacrifice[6]. More so, all three also fulfill Kolker's requirement that self-sacrifice be something that either occurs in secret or through inaction (181). In all three series, especially *Buffy* and *Supernatural*, the characters are acting out of the public spotlight. Mulder and Scully operate out of a basement office or outside official FBI channels; Buffy's tombstone, which proclaims that "she saved the world a lot," is hidden from view in a secluded glen; and Sam and Dean constantly work under aliases out of random hotel rooms as they cross the country looking for evil things to smite.

For all their emotion and melodramatic action, *The X-Files*, *Buffy*, and *Supernatural* each began somewhat quietly and were not expected to last long, largely because of their focus on paranormal and supernatural themes. All three touch on subjects that are mysterious

---

[6] The frequency of these sacrifices is something to be considered in the conclusion. Mulder makes small sacrifices all the time, but *The X-Files* stays away from world-shattering sacrificial moments every season. *Buffy* and *Supernatural*, however, both have a life and death sacrifice moment at least once every season. It's almost expected, so there is the risk that these sacrifices could lose their significance over time.

or unknown, and all three invoke religion – the sacred and profane, alien and external – and question its purpose in our lives. The fan response, however, kept the shows in rotation. *The X-Files* ran for nine seasons, *Buffy* for seven seasons, and *Supernatural* is currently in its ninth season with negotiations for a tenth. The characters and situations have become part of mainstream pop culture to the point that even if a person never watched an episode, he or she would likely understand a reference to Buffy, Mulder and Scully or the Winchester brothers.

It is my belief that these three shows serve as a good vehicle for the exploration of the trend of Common Christs replacing traditional Christ figures. *The X-Files* launched a new fervor of conspiracy mania with its constant questioning of "the powers that be," and what it means to have faith in a concept. Though it had only a few episodes that dealt directly with religious themes, correlations can be made between the distrust of the governing body and personal belief and the religious shift America has been undergoing for the last 20-25 years. The Church – as a ruling organization of communal ritual – is pitted against the private, personal belief system of the individual. And as opinions and beliefs of the Church change, so do interpretations and perceptions of religious icons. In this fluctuating religious landscape then, *Buffy* and *Supernatural* specifically bring out the move away from the one-and-done savior aspect of Christ into the idea of repeated salvation made possible through the acts of common people.

The Common Christ is a reflection of America's discomfort with being saved by a perfect savior, of owing a debt that, in Christian terms, it can never repay. Religiously speaking, Christ has evolved from an ethereal being into a common, every-day person like us. Where the Christ of old was described as an enigma by St. Augustine or something viewed as "through a glass, darkly" by St. Paul, the new, American Christ (as will be seen in the next chapter) is a friend who "walks with me and talks with me" (Erickson 112).[7] A new

creature for a high/low culture, Christ is merely a "20th century American whose principal

difference is that he has already risen from the dead" (Bloom, *Post-Christian Nation* 65). The

Common Christ takes this American Christ even further; instead of appearing to be the savior

of all who asks nothing in return, the Common Christs in *The X-Files, Buffy,* and

Supernatural (often reluctantly) work out of a love for close family and friends, not the world

as a whole.

All three shows also share a common bond in their ties to supernatural, paranormal,

and Gothic themes. According to Victoria Nelson in *Gothicka: Vampire Heroes, Human*

Gods, and the New Supernatural, the supernatural has long been linked to the Gothic

tradition, even if the modern Gothic works to explain the supernatural more often than not.[8]

Specifically, though, the Gothic is often recognized as being an area of exploration and

questioning of the supernatural nature of religion and faith. Nelson argues that, during the

Englightenment, early Gothic operated "in the vacuum left by the departure of religious

beliefs among large portions of the educated classes" (10-11), and Victor Sage in *Horror*

Fiction in the Protestant Tradition claims that the Gothic genre features a "whole complex of

popular theological ideals of a predominantly, if not exclusively Protestant variety" (as qtd.

in Nelson 11). As the Gothic has evolved, "the genre of supernatural horror has been the

preferred mode," according to Nelson, that "a pre-dominantly secular scientific culture such

---

[7] 1 Corinthians 13:12: "For now we see through a glass, darkly; but then face to face: now I know in part; but then shall I know even as also I am known." Paul is commenting on the state of human knowledge being incomplete, saying we do not have a clear image of God/Jesus now, but "then" – once heaven is achieved – the image will be clear and known.

[8] This is not to say that traditional Gothic works never explained the supernatural; there are several Enlightenment Gothic works, such as Anne Radcliffe's *Mysteries of Udolpho* (1794), or Charles Brockden Brown's *Wieland* (1798), that work to explain the supernatural.

as ours has had for imagining and encountering the sacred" when such questioning has been

denied by the actual governing body of the church (xi).

This inability (or sometimes just the lack of a desire) to question religious authority is

another reason to focus on shows that are not necessarily classified as "religious shows."

Programs that have an obvious religious basis, such as *Highway to Heaven, Touched by an*

Angel, or even those that have an edgier, more contemporary version of Christianity such as

Joan of Arcadia or *Saving Grace*, are more likely to draw an audience with traditional views

of religion. Even though they deal specifically with Christianity, and each of these programs

could fit into my discussion of the disappearance of the traditional Christ figure – none of

them have Christ as a character/figure on the show, and most of them avoid mentioning

Christ at all. *Joan of Arcadia* and *Saving Grace* also have characters who fulfill the role of

Common Christs, but shows without direct religious affiliation are more representative of the

shift away from organized religion to personal faith. They explore and profess many of the

same tenets as these Christianity-based programs, but *Supernatural, Buffy,* and *The X-Files*

also bring in a mix of views, practices and beliefs that I feel are partially responsible for this

transition from traditional Christ figures into Common Christs.

The Truth is Out There

In 1992, Harold Bloom called America a "religion mad" nation, saying that

"[Americans] have revised the traditional religion into a faith that better fits our national

temperament, aspirations, and anxieties" (*The American Religion* 45). This revision has made

Americans less dependent upon the organization of religion – the church and Christ – for

salvation, instead sending us in search of our own personal expressions of faith. In this

dissertation, that search begins in the next chapter, "Let's Talk about Jesus: Differentiating

Christ Figures and Common Christs," with a clarification of the definition of the Christ figure, as well as a discussion of the function of Christ figures in modern texts culminating in the introduction of what I call the Common Christ. The next chapter, "*The X-Files* and Christ: The Truth is Out There" is a brief discussion of how this character appears in one of the seminal text of *The X-Files*, a show responsible for the success of both *Buffy* and *Supernatural*. The third chapter, "*Buffy, the Vampire Slayer* - Just a Girl: the Savior in a Micro-Mini," will examine that Common Christ as it appears in *Buffy* and the show's treatment of Christianity. Then, the Common Christ theme will be examined in Dean and Sam Winchester in the chapter, "'If I do not save everyone, then no one will, and we all die':" Death, Sacrifice, and Christianity in *Supernatural*." Both chapters dealing with *Buffy* and *Supernatural* focus on the paradox of having a storyline based in Christian mythos that does not necessarily embrace Christianity. Finally, in the conclusion, I discuss how this evolution of the Christ figure into a Common Christ, one who takes salvation from a perfect being and puts it into the hands of an imperfect common man, represents a shift not only in how we receive these characters but also in how we produce their stories. The expectation is that this will open a larger discussion on the authority of popular culture in deeply held, core belief systems.

Chapter One: Let's Talk About Jesus:

Differentiating Christ Figures and Common Christs

Let's Talk About Jesus

"Hi, I'd like to talk to you about Jesus Christ…"

In America today, this simple statement can produce a variety of reactions ranging in emotion from apathy to strong passion. More often than not, the response is one of uncertainty, even if we happen to agree with the religious outlook of the speaker. We are afraid to be drawn into the conversation because of the current status that organized religion holds in America and, as such, would just rather avoid the discussion. For example, a friend, whose husband suffers from Crohn's Disease, told me a story about a recent doctor's visit. During the post-exam discussion, the topic somehow moved into the realm of religion. The doctor began speaking of her own personal faith and religious beliefs and my friend became quite uncomfortable with the discussion. Even though she'd just watched the doctor perform invasive medical procedures on her husband without feeling the least bit bashful or unsure, the mere mention of religion made her hesitant about how to proceed with the conversation.

This discomfort is not only limited to one-on-one conversations; it is also present in the mass realm of entertainment. The mere use of the word God is sometimes considered more offensive or uncomfortable than basic profanity. When a program or film airs on television that contains profanity, those words are bleeped out or dubbed with a less offensive version. Cultural evolution has now deemed certain profanity to be less offensive than the rest, so some words slip through that might have been bleeped in years prior, like "damn" or "hell."[1] If the program has the phrase "God damn it," however, we are dealing

---

[1] Aside from a change in cultural responses to profanity, there has been a general push against network standards since the United States Supreme Court has ruled against the FCC in recent years, limiting their power

with a new area. The "damn it" is no longer deemed offensive, but the presence of "God" in

front of it changes the meaning of the phrase. The religious terminology has made it more

profane than the uttering of "damn it" to an unnamed, unspecified deity we hope will reign

damnation down upon whoever or whatever is vexing us. But instead of bleeping the entire

phrase, most censor programs will bleep out "God" and allow the "damn it" part of the

phrase to go through. Other shows and networks have censored "Jesus" from broadcasts if it

was being used in anything other than sincere praise.[2] As a society, we are more comfortable

with profanity than God and the Christian religion, partly because we know what to do with

profanity, what it means and what's expected when we use it. God and Christianity, however,

are murkier concepts.

As Americans, we love to tout our basic rights as presented in the First Amendment,

especially the rights to freedom of speech and religion. But we have a small space in which

we willingly allow those two rights to collide. Ideally, we respect each other's rights to free

speech and worship, as long as someone does not use free speech to try and talk to us about

religion. For all our freedom to choose which religion to practice, religious expression in

mainstream American society is actually quite restricted. As the story of my friend's doctor

visit and the discussion of God and profanity on TV have shown, we are willing to talk about

almost anything else aside from religion.

---

to fine networks for airing profanity and nudity. Also, I am talking about regular network TV at this point.
Shows on cable channels like FX or USA Network (not just HBO or Showtime, long known for pushing the
envelope) allow even more profanity to air.

[2] Most notably, the shows *Duck Dynasty* and *The View* have dealt with this issue. In a rebroadcast of an episode
of *The View*, one cast member's playful phrase of "thank you, thank you Jesus" had "Jesus" bleeped out, even
though it ran in the live broadcast. In *Duck Dynasty*, according to an interview Phil Robertson gave to Stephen
Copeland with *Sports Spectrum*, A&E bleeped out "in Jesus' name" from the end of the family prayers. There
has also been controversy about the show adding in censor bleeps in post-production when it first ran to make it
sound as if cast members were cursing (even if they were not). The bleeps were added to make the show seem
more like other reality shows.

Despite this widespread discomfort, religion has permeated much of American culture. We see it on our money – "In God We Trust"; we say it in the Pledge of Allegiance – "one nation, under God"; we sing it on the steps of government buildings in times of crisis – "God Bless America." It is still common practice in most courts to swear in testimony with a Bible and the oath, "to tell the truth, the whole truth and nothing but the truth, so help you God." Christmas and Easter – two of the largest Christian holidays – are considered national/government holidays. And yet we eagerly ban prayer in schools. We cry foul whenever courthouses display copies of the Ten Commandments, citing the ever popular "separation of church and state." It is not that we don't recognize the presence of the Church, specifically Christianity (almost all the major references to religion in government documents, pledges and songs directly reference or proclaim a Christian God – one and only, capital G) within our government in all those other forms. But this presence is in ways we've long internalized and accepted as being part of American culture rather than being a sign of religious obedience.

Most, if not all of these religious incarnations were established during a time of strong religious fervor. They are conventional, memorized and we often speak the words without even recognizing them as being religious in nature. We like the concept of being blessed, of being watched over by a supreme being. We just don't like the idea of organized Religion (imposing, with a capital R, as opposed to the smaller, personal religion) that goes with it. God bless America, indeed.

As such, we have a somewhat bi-polar relationship with religion in America. We have accepted the notion that our nation was founded on Christian principles, but we do not like it when it "shoves" Christianity down our throats. We are not thrilled when other religions are highlighted, either, but Christianity bears the brunt of rejection. This rejection is

not just seen in response to elements of government and civic life, but also in the rise of non-

denominational congregations. Americans are leaving traditional denominational

organizations in favor of congregations that may share some of the tenets of traditional

churches but are not quite as binding or rule-bound. In his review of data on religious

affiliations in America, Scott Thuma found that around 12.2 million Americans identify

themselves as attending nondenominational churches, making them the third largest religious

group in the United States.[3] Thuma also reports that when looking at data collected by the

American Religious Identification Survey (2008), Barry Kosmin found the number of self-

identifying nondenominational Protestants had greatly increased from previous surveys,

saying, "the rise of non-denominational Christianity is probably one of the strongest trends in

the last two decades … . It is nearly as sharp an increase as the no-religion response." This

shift has led to an increase in people identifying as spiritual or as having a personal

faithrather than identifying with a specific religion. [4] Part of the reason for this exodus from

traditional churches is because Americans have lost faith in the institutions of religion as

more and more stories of corrupt church practices or officials have come to light, along with

the church's inflexibility on issues (e.g. divorce, gay marriage, abortion) that are becoming

more acceptable to a growing majority of Americans.

This shift away from organized religion has manifested in a change in the

representation of Christianity in mainstream entertainment. As more people separate

themselves from specific religious affiliations in favor of nondenominational ones, a schism

---

[3] Nondenominational churches are third behind Roman Catholic and Southern Baptist groups (Thuma).
[4] A sense of "personal faith" can be defined as a set of religious beliefs that may or may not conform to a
traditional dogma. The individual has created their own faith and belief, choosing what they will or will not
follow in regards to church teachings.

has developed between religious material and audiences. While we accept that many of our favorite stories have a foundation in Christian mythos – the horror industry, with its demon possession/exorcism stories or apocalyptic prophecy films, often relies heavily on Christianity/religion, for example – we're not so accepting of material that is billed specifically as Christian-based or Christian-inspired. Even though the highest grossing Christian film, *The Passion of the Christ* (2004) pulled in over $370 million dollars, that is not quite half the proceeds of James Cameron's blockbuster *Avatar* (2009), which had a Christ figure as its hero, but was not billed as a Christ-tale.

The same apathy towards Christian-based entertainment is more easily seen in the lack of successful television shows that have a blatant or specific tie-in with Christianity. Successful shows with a specific Christian ideology, like *Highway to Heaven* (1984-1989) or *Touched by an Angel* (1994-2003), are few and far between. Usually, openly Christian television programs do not last long on the air. Even programs that are not promoting a warm and fuzzy, light and fluffy view of Christianity, like *Saving Grace* (2007-2010), have a hard time holding enough viewers to keep from getting the axe. Grace, the title character, is a hard drinking, promiscuous cop who develops her faith through intermittent visits from a scruffy, tobacco spitting angel named Earl. Another example would be *Joan of Arcadia* (2003-2005), a re-telling of the Joan of Arc story with Joan as a typical American teenager who literally speaks to God (as opposed to an angel, like Grace) and performs tasks he sets her. *Joan of Arcadia* does differ from most short-run religious themed shows in that it had a devoted, if small, fan following despite its network cancellation.

The low audience ratings and subsequent cancellation of these types of shows do not happen because we do not want to see Christian ethos on television. We do – several of our long-running series portray it. We just do not think of them as being overly Christian. Instead, we see the display of morality as part of the storyline, and the Christ figure (if we recognize it as Christ) as a metaphor for personal sacrifice and not the image of a religious savior. Given a choice, the majority of people will prefer to watch a program that may be Christian in its leanings but does not advertise itself as such, as opposed to actively seeking out Christian programming (Horner as qtd in Berg). For example, *The Twilight Zone*, a series that was not only popular in its time but has also become something of a cult favorite, is not considered religious, yet a majority of the storylines portray basic morality tales that pull from the Christian standard. Other examples, like *Lois & Clark* and *Smallville,* show strong Christ-like figures of sacrifice in Clark Kent/Superman. Shows like these may reference religion (either directly or indirectly), but they are not actively *advocating* belief in religion.

Religious tautology exists in entertainment without our direct notice because we are used to it being there. We want to keep seeing it because, as an audience, we like "convergence and repetition. We find security by having the same stories told over and over again" (Kolker 150).[5] Like our reactions to "In God we Trust," we have internalized the basic tenets of Christianity in American society so that, unless something is marketed specifically as being Christian in nature, we see these expressions more as a cultural choice than a religious belief. We do not have to be believers in the faith in order to follow or be affected by the religious metaphors because they have been given relevance outside religion. Even if the creators, writers and producers do not identify as overly Christian, they may express

---

[5] This theory of convergence also explains why similar themes show up in various mythologies and the lasting popularity of genre-based entertainment.

Christian mythology in their work because they are responding to a cultural pull.[6] Theodore

Ziolkowski, author of *Fictional Transfigurations of Jesus*, claims this relevance comes from

the gospel stories being transformed into a "cultural possession" that does not require the

audience to share a faith or religious belief in order to recognize and appreciate them

(*Fictional Transfigurations* viii). Because religious metaphors and ethos are now cultural

possessions, they become less threatening as markers of religion. We still recognize them as

religious, but when used as metaphors by mainstream media instead of being preached by

marketed-religious programming, they cease to be "religion," itself.

Thus, we find the mirror of the shift from traditional churches to nondenominational

congregations in the social acceptance of religious metaphor outside religion. As I mentioned

before, people who are dissatisfied with organized religions are leaving the doubt, corruption

and binding rules behind for more open worship experiences that offer opportunities for the

growth and experience of personal faith. Part of the reason they do not abandon religious

faith altogether is because, as Yi-Fu Tuan explains in *Religion: From Place to Placelessness*,

religion is essential for group cohesion and identity; it makes people feel "at home" in the

world (34). Whether they are consciously remaining faithful out of a desire to maintain their

identity or not does not matter – inherently, they realize the role of faith and belief in regard

to making a place for themselves within a culture, of maintaining that "cultural possession"

Ziolkowski discusses. For Tuan, it is not necessarily about the religious experience in terms

of faith and belief – it is the cultural experience that counts. Therefore, it makes sense that we

---

[6] Some authors/producers specifically identify as atheist or agnostic, and yet they still have strong Christian
themes in their work. A notable example is Joss Whedon, creator of *Buffy, the Vampire Slayer*. Whedon is
openly atheist, yet he has created a world that relies heavily on Christian mythology and ethos, and characters
who frequently establish themselves as Christ figures and figures of sacrifice. Whedon has admitted in
interviews that he has not made these choices consciously with Christianity in mind, but that they were story-
telling decisions that happen to line up with Christian mythology. He is a prime example of Ziolkowski's idea
of "cultural possession" and Kolker's theory of convergence.

would welcome Christian ethos in our stories even if we did not want religion in them because with the addition of these metaphors and symbols, "even the simplest folklore theme becomes enlarged, illuminated and marvelously transformed" (Campbell, *The Mythic Image* 479). Thus, religious references in entertainment become something common without being an explicit religious declaration or attempt at conversion.

Who Are We Talking about Again?

Knowing American television is rife with Christ figures and religious references does not mean that we all see the same Christ figure or envision the same Christ when he is referenced. American Christianity is evolving, and with it the expectations of who Christ is, both within and outside the church, and what he can do. It is not the scope of this project to outline every transition of the figure of Christ in American Christianity and trace the impact of these changes on entertainment. There are, however, resources that trace this evolution. Stephen Prothero's *American Jesus: How the Son of God Became a National Icon* (2003) is an excellent resource for examining the various ways Jesus has changed or has been changed to meet specific needs of the Church in America. Prothero traces transformations of dogma, doctrine, and image throughout American history to show how Jesus has become an important figure in American Christianity to the point that he is now a pop-culture icon. In their book, *America's Four Gods: What We Say About God – And What That Says About Us* (2010), sociologists Paul Forese and Christopher Bader briefly examine not only the evolving nature of Jesus and God in American Christianity, but also how those views can reveal our attitudes on other social issues, such as politics, justice, war and science, to name a few.

Paul Boyer's article, "Two Centuries of Christianity in America: An Overview" (2001) also offers a brief but thorough discussion of the evolution of Christ as a figurehead and American Christianity, with a broader view available in Mark A. Noll's *The Old Religion in a New World: The History of North American Christianity* (2002). In his book, Noll not only traces the history of Christianity in America, but looks at its roots in Europe and how it evolves in both Canada and Mexico, giving us more points of comparison. Alan Wolfe's *The Transformation of American Religion: How We Actually Live Our Faith* (2003) goes in the opposite direction by pinpointing specific examples of how Protestantism has changed in America. Wolfe breaks his work into overarching themes, but focuses the discussion within those chapters on individual churches and leaders to show how those themes are changing and evolving in society. And, of course, no discussion of American Christianity would be complete without mentioning Harold Bloom's prolific works on religion, including *Jesus and Yahweh: The Names Divine* (2005) and *The Book of J* (1990). Most notable is his book *The American Religion*, first published in 1992 and then republished in a new edition, *The American Religion: The Emergence of the Post-Christian Nation* in 2006. Including discussions of Mormonism, Jehovah's Witnesses and other American-born faiths, *The American Religion* does not focus specifically on Christianity, but it does offer a framework for understanding the American attitude towards religion (including Christianity), as well as looking at the role religion plays in American culture.

It is important to determine the current position of Christ as a figure in American culture so as to better understand how the depiction of Christ figures is changing. An easy way to establish this cultural view is by looking at how we visually portray God and Christ. According to Froese and Bader's study, Americans are fairly equally split in a mental image of God as being one of four options: Authoritative, Benevolent, Critical or Distant. More often, however, we lump those four into two separate entities – one who is caring and protective, or distant and judging. Whichever category he is placed in, the Christian God is often depicted as being somewhat separated from the rhythms of modern society. He is presented either as a kindly old man with a long white beard in a toga or robe (perhaps reminiscent of Santa Claus on sabbatical), or as a distant figure, aged and removed from the realities of life on Earth as he basks in angelic adoration in heaven. The jolly-old-elf God often comes across as mystified by the complexities of the modern world, while still remaining as the constant companion and protector. Recently, those who see him as benevolent have begun to demystify and personalize him, seeing him more as just the *Abba* – daddy and teacher, father and forgiver – as opposed to an all-powerful being. The vengeful, jealous version of God, sometimes referred to as the Old Testament God, is envisioned as aloof, not needing to reach out to Man for worship because he is assured of his position as the "one, true God." For those who follow this view of God, he is less the patient *Abba* father-figure and more like the absent father, looking down from on high, ready to judge and condemn mankind for its failings.

The dual perception of the presence and identity of a Christian God, however, is nothing when compared to the cultural abjection we seem to hold for Jesus Christ. Where the Christian God proclaims Himself exalted above all others, Christ makes salvation even narrower by establishing himself as the only way to heaven – "I am *the* Way, *the* Truth and *the* Life. No one comes to the father *except* through Me" (emphasis added, John 14:6). It is not just that Christ is *a* way of salvation, He is *the* one and only way. If that were not enough to set Him apart, Jesus is also presented as blameless, the perfect, sinless human being. He is the kid we all hated in school – the teacher's pet who can do no wrong, and always does as he's told. He represents rules and boundaries and regulation. On the other hand, he is also the gentle Lamb, the willing sacrifice and selfless intercessor. He has been adopted by both conservatives and liberals – he is socialism and capitalism, fundamental and liberal. He can be difficult to recognize as the same figure.

Culturally, Christ has also become something of an icon in American society. Where God seems distant and out of step with modern society, Jesus is a "fixture on the American landscape," appearing on billboards, bumper stickers and even as tattoos (Prothero, *American Jesus* 11). There is a theme park – The Holy Land Experience – in Orlando, Florida; the Merritt Ministry out of Tracy, California has a 110-foot tall hot-air balloon in the shape of Jesus in a purple robe; Jesus has been the focus of two flashy musicals, *Godspell* (1971) and *Jesus Christ, Superstar* (1971); in 2012, Facebook and Lightside Games started *Journey of Jesus: The Calling*, an online role-playing game which invites people to travel alongside Jesus through the Gospels and "walk in the Messiah's steps" (Newcomb); and internet memes exist showing Jesus talking to a group of superheroes and explaining how he "saved the world" or invoking him in nerd culture with the phrase: "Jesus saves, Allah forgives, and Cthulhu thinks you taste good with ketchup" alongside depictions of Jesus as a zombie. Christ has changed from an abstract concept of religion into "a personality, a celebrity, and finally an icon" (Prothero, *American Jesus* 12). He has become such a cultural figure that invoking the figure or name of Jesus Christ does not automatically invoke the traditional, dogmatic Christ of Christianity. One has to examine the cultural context of the reference to understand just which one we are trying to emulate when we ask, "what would Jesus do?"

Common Christs – Reflecting the Common Man

Whether meant as a religious motif or simply as a stock character of sacrifice, a Christ figure carries with it a huge cultural weight. Christ figures, essentially, are suggestions of Christ within a character. These figures are traditionally spiritual or prophetic characters who parallel Christ in some form. Traditional Christ figures are usually martyrs, willingly sacrificing themselves for larger causes, sometimes resurrected to fully complete the embodiment of Christ, though that is not a requirement. In America, Christ figures were encouraged by the church because it was a way to make the figure of Jesus popular while also making use of fiction to make religion more entertaining, thereby hopefully drawing in more to the congregation (Prothero, *American Jesus* 64). The authors creating Christ figures went along with it because it was a way to have the work of novels and writing deemed respectable by the Church (65). Many early Christ figures tended to have JC as initials, or at the very least, a first name that began with J in order to make their connection to Jesus Christ more complete.

A point to clarify is that there are such characters as Jesus figures alongside Christ figures, but they are not the same, just as Jesus the man is not the same as Christ. Jesus of Nazareth is a historical figure who, by being identified as the Christ, begins the Christian religion. He is The Christ, but when we refer to Christ as a figure, we are invoking the theological sign, a title. Christ is not his given name (Prothero, *American Jesus* 9). Ziolkowski explains this difference by categorizing the life of Jesus in the Gospels as being something that remains constant, whereas Christ becomes kerygmatic.[7]

Jesus figures are characters that are specifically meant to represent Jesus. Ziolkowski calls these characters "fictional transfigurations," and clarifies that rather than just being

---

[7] The *kerygma* is the connotation of Christ and his works developed by the Christian faith (Ziolkowski, *Fictional Transfigurations* 9). According to Ziolkowski, this trend of separation between Jesus and Christ began with Saint Paul's writings about Christ (*Fictional Transfigurations* 31). Paul's interpretation of Christ is not based on personal knowledge and acquaintance with Jesus. Instead, he focuses on the *kerygma* of the resurrected Christ, thereby furthering the separation between Jesus and Christ and establishing Christ, the savior, as the foundation of the Christian religion instead of Jesus.

inspired by Christ's role of sacrifice, they are "prefigured to a noticeable extent by figures and events popularly associated with the life of Jesus as it is known from the Gospels" (*Fictional Transfigurations* 6). The action, imagery and organization of the story lines surrounding these characters are directly borrowed from the biblically recorded life of Jesus. Christ figures, however are not required to mirror Jesus' life at all. They simply must fulfill a role of sacrifice and possible salvation. Edwin Moseley calls these characters "pseudonyms of Christ," and F.W. Dillistone describes them as characters "ready to accept suffering and even death in the service of a transcendent value, a worthy end" (as qtd in Ziolkowski, *Fictional Transfigurations* 26-27). Christ figures function as the messiah in the text – the method of salvation and redemption through sacrifice regardless of whether their lives mirror that of Jesus at any other point.

Christ is an easy model of sacrifice for traditional heroes because, as far as characters go, he is a flat, one-dimensional character. He has only one driving goal – to sacrifice himself in the place of sinners and to fulfill his Father's plan of salvation for humanity. If one looks at his prayers in the garden of Gethsemane, where he prays to have the task of dying on the cross taken away from him, or perhaps his cry while on the cross asking why God has forsaken him, he may become two-dimensional. He's allowed to question God briefly, but in the end, he does as required. He does not buck the system or go off script. This kind of selfless drive is easy to instill in a character. It does not require a long series of exposition or explanation. Looking at the bible as literature, Christ does not offer long, character-driven explanations for his actions or beliefs. He simply references God, his Father, and claims to be doing His work. Likewise, traditional Christ figures can simply be displayed as driven and loyal, to the point of death, for a cause and we accept their actions in fulfilment of that drive.

The Christ figure is changing, however, because the culture in which he has to function is changing, much as Christ evolved to keep up with the evolution of American Christianity. Ziolkowski claims that depictions of Christ must evolve to "reflect the vagaries of society's image of the culture-hero Jesus" (viii). Part of this change is simply a response to new ways of telling stories and expectations of character, but a larger part is because of the changed cultural view of Christ. We have moved from static Christ figures who, even though they may not have reflected the events of Jesus' life, were often depicted as moral, upstanding figures, to Christ figures who are more in line with the common man – Common Christs.

Religious critic Vincent Ferrer Blehl in "Literature and Religious Belief," says that the author/creator of the Christ figure is "free, of course, to make whatever he wishes of the Christ figure," and that "the Christ figure of American [media] is not one with the Christ of the believer" (308). I would argue, however, that Common Christs often do function as examples of contemporary Christian belief. It seems improbable, after all, that our religious image of Christ should not resemble, at least in part, our cultural image, or vice versa.

The stories we tell illuminate our opinions, our beliefs, and our culture, from overarching ideals of government to small, everyday patterns. The characters in these stories are not the products of individual imaginations, though they each bear the individual touch of the person who created them; they are the products of cultural contexts (Kolker 117). Simply put, the villains represent common fears and worries while the heroes represent cultural ideals and aspirations. When our villains exhibit signs of humanity or our heroes are hesitant to perform, they reflect crises in the prevailing culture (Ziolkowski, *Hesitant Heroes* 4). But does this apply to our Christ figures? Christ is depicted as a savior, a redeemer – he is also a hero.

In his seminal work *Hero with a Thousand Faces*, Joseph Campbell explains that the hero is someone who has moved beyond all limitations; he has died as a modern man but has been brought back as "an eternal man – perfected, unspecific, universal" (19-20). The hero is someone who goes on a journey, encounters fantastic forces and returns victorious with power or a message to give to the people (30). For Campbell, there is no question that Christ is a hero figure – as are many other religious figures he mentions throughout the work, both inside and outside Christianity. Christ functions as a universal hero of the world and has several moments within the gospels where he completes mini-heroic deeds that identify him as a hero.[8] While not all heroes are Christ figures, it is safe to say that all Christ figures are heroes in some sense because they act with the sole intent of redeeming or saving some aspect of society. If our heroes change to reflect cultural views, then it stands to reason that when Christ figures change, they do so as a representation of a change in the understanding of Christ both as a cultural and a religious figure.[9]

In the case of Christ and Christ figures, there is a changing interpretation both religiously and culturally. Religiously, we have slowly been working to demystify Christ – to make him known and relatable, someone we can understand. A common religious children's song says: "I wish I had a little white box/ to put my Jesus in./ I'd take him out and kiss, kiss,

---

[8] As an example, Campbell describes the Transfiguration of Christ in Matthew 17:1-9 as being a mini version of the monomyth within Christ's entire heroic journey. He guides Peter, James and John away from the common world to the mountaintop; he encounters the spectral versions of Moses and Elias; and then he returns to the disciples with a message.

[9] This is not to say that the Christ figure – be it traditional or a Common Christ – has replaced the Christ of Christianity. I understand Blehl's point about Christ figures not representing Christian belief. The Christ figure is a symbol, a "vehicle of communication" as Campbell calls it (*The Hero with A Thousand Faces* 236). What I am arguing is that even though the Christ figure does not replace Christ, the opinions and interpretations of Christ from believers and society do influence the Christ figures we get in stories. They change as we do.

kiss/ and put him back again." We wish we could easily categorize Christ, put him in a box. Traditional Christ figures, though simple and one-dimensional as far as characters go, were still examples of the religious interpretation of Christ in that we did not always understand the motivations behind their sacrifice. Like Christ in the Bible, they simply fulfill the role of martyr out of a sense of love or duty. Jim Casy, in Steinbeck's *The Grapes of Wrath*, for example, is a "mythic expression of the immense human love … for his fellow man" (Ziolkowski, *Fictional Transifigurations* 188), but his transformation into such an expression is something we do not fully understand.

The same is true for Aslan from C.S. Lewis' *The Lion, The Witch and the Wardrobe*. Love is what takes him to death, as with Jim Casy, but even more mysteriously, he is resurrected through the powers of an old magic that stems from "before the dawn of time."[10] There are still mysticism and supernatural elements at work that are never explained, leaving us uncertain as to how sacrifice and salvation work. This desire to demystify Christ is partially why Common Christs are usually explained as much as possible. We have elaborate backstories and origins for their actions; if they are resurrected, we generally see the method of it. Even if the origin story or resurrection is supernatural in nature, we are given a breakdown of the spell or the power hierarchy used to accomplish this. Common Christs are tangible and known in a way that traditional Christ figures are not.

This is especially true for Common Christs in fringe and cult TV shows. Because *The X-Files, Buffy,* and *Supernatural* are part of the supernatural/horror genre, all the supernatural or paranormal elements are easier to swallow because we have already accepted the fantastic

---

[10] This is the phrase used in C.S. Lewis' *The Lion, The Witch and the Wardrobe* to describe when the old magics were created. There is also a chapter within the work, Chapter 15, entitled, "Deeper Magic from Before the Dawn of Time."

nature of the worlds depicted. We follow these characters through encounters with ghosts, demons, aliens and other phantasmagoria, watching them retrieve and collect evidence. We listen to their research and see them consult books and tomes and case-files. We are not just told that a ritual will resurrect someone before the ritual takes place – we get ingredient lists and discussions about why one ingredient in particular is important over another. For the first three seasons of *Buffy*, one of the main sets is a library, a place of knowledge and learning. Sam and Dean of *Supernatural* do not just randomly try methods of killing demons. They have a system and guides – their dad's journal for one, or the books of lore at their mentor Bobby's house for another. Mulder and Scully work for the FBI – they are trained to detect information. They have access to forensic labs to examine evidence. Even when Mulder spouts something that sounds incredibly unlikely, he has documentation to support his claims in the form of testimony, photos, sound recordings and, sometimes, physical evidence. He has filing cabinets full of information. The fact that there are case-files matters. This is not some random, spooky occurrence. Even if it is labeled an "X-file," there's still documentation. These shows work to explain the supernatural elements as much as possible instead of simply using the supernatural as a *deus ex machina*.

Culturally, Common Christs are responding to the American psyche. The American Dream and American ego are all about independence. The myth of the American is of an individual who pulls himself up by his bootstraps, strikes out and explores, and survives the vast frontier – independently and alone as opposed to bound by society. The myth of America is that of a country not beholden to someone or something. The concepts of American Exceptionalism and Manifest Destiny allow for the idea of being blessed, of being special, but this is not the same as being personally indebted to someone, especially someone who is perfect in a way that we can never be. The sinless, perfect Christ is unobtainable and, in dying for the sins of the world, he sets up a tab that we can never fully pay back. And so, we set about making Christ as human as possible, keeping him as a model of behavior without necessarily having to accept his ascetic way of life (Campbell, *The Hero of a Thousand Faces* 320). A Common Christ – one who acts like us, speaks like us, and thinks like us – is not a symbol of perfection. A Common Christ is accessible and therefore can be repaid.[11] Even if a Common Christ is superhuman in some way – Buffy for example – he/she is still more accessible because she gives into her human nature and can conceivably be reimbursed through human means.

Another reason we are drawn to Common Christs is because of the way humanity is viewed in comparison to them as opposed to a traditional, sinless Christ. In religious terms, humanity is born sinful and impure, headed for hellfire and damnation if not for the salvation of God. Traditionally, that salvation could come in the form of humanity dangling over hell by a thin strand of spiderweb (as described in Jonathan Edwards' *Sinners in the Hands of an Angry God*), or the loving, gentle hand of Christ knocking at the door of our hearts. With Common Christs, however, humanity is on the same level as the savior.[12] The Common Christ and humanity come from the same background and therefore are on the same level in terms of guilt and innocence. The Common Christs in *The X-Files*, *Buffy*, and *Supernatural*,

---

[11] This is also part of why organized religions focus so much on rituals – they offer us a formula. If we do [fill in the blank], then we will receive what we ask for, be it love, forgiveness, blessing, or any number of other things. This is also why new churches, both traditional and nondenominational, have started a trend of having empty crosses in place of crucifixes. Some are getting rid of the cross altogether (Prothero, *American Jesus* 150). The crucifix and the empty cross both represent the debt owed for salvation.

[12] This is not to say that Christ or traditional Christ figures are not human. The human nature of Christ has long been a subject of contention in the Church. But as has been previously stated, even though Christ is human, he is a perfect human – one without sin. There is no such thing elsewhere in humanity, so having a Common Christ – one who is on the same level – is a change. It is true that the New Testament and modern Christianity emphasizes the "lost sheep" aspect of humanity as opposed to the "dirty sinners hanging over hell" aspect, but Christ is still being displayed as the perfect, sinless being.

all mention the equality of humanity and their worthiness of salvation. Mulder constantly pushes for full disclosure of information, saying that people deserve to know "the truth." And even though Dean often says "people suck," he, Sam, and Buffy fight to protect "the innocent" people who do not deserve to be eaten, maimed, killed or sucked into the random hell dimension of the week.

Common Christs are not just invested in protecting and saving people – they are people. Sam and Dean, Mulder and Scully, Buffy and her friends deal not only with the weight of the world on a weekly basis, but with regular human problems as well. Sam wants to go to college; Buffy wants a date; Mulder deals with worries at work. They deal with issues that we, the audience, are familiar with. Their responses to the world are also human. Culturally, Christ and traditional Christ figures are cast as pious and righteous. In modern terms, we translate this to mean that Christ is boring. Religion tries to set Christ up as being all inclusive and welcoming, yet because he is "*the* way" of salvation, he is seen as being exclusive. Christ and Christianity are laws, boundaries, rules and commandments – they are controlling and limiting. Common Christs not only tend to break the rules, or at the very least go against conventions, but they have fun while doing so. They drink, they party, and they date.

Another reason we are drawn to Common Christs is because they fly in the face of authority, both in terms of the Church and their storylines. Buffy defies the Watchers' Council, in essence the purveyors of religion in Buffy's world, for several seasons before officially breaking with them and not having any contact with them unless it is on her terms.[13] Mulder and Scully confront different authority figures ranging from the mundane to

clandestine, as well as taking on the church itself in a few episodes. Sam and Dean perhaps

embody this idea of defiance the best because they do not merely challenge some metaphor

or representative of the church. Starting in the fourth season and beyond, they are dealing

with God and all his angels directly. Not only does Dean refuse to aid God and Heaven by

being a vessel for the archangel Michael, he and Sam routinely comment on the strictness of

angels and religion, going so far as to refer to angels constantly as "dicks," and other colorful

names. We are drawn to these characters because they are willing to stand up to beings,

entities, and institutions much bigger and stronger than they are. They are willing to call

attention to the hypocrisy of these authorities.[14] As such, they give us another reason to root

for them outside of their heroic deeds to save the world. We respect them not only for their

hero status – we celebrate their humanness.

These Common Christs are common not just in their humanity, but also in the

frequency of their appearances. In "The Work of Art in the Age of Mechanical

Reproduction," Walter Benjamin argues that, in an age of mass culture and mass

reproduction, anything capable of being reproduced has "lost that which makes it special,

even worthy of worship" (as qtd in Kolker 124). Benjamin calls this special quality an

object's aura. Because everyone is able to have the same exact product through mass

reproduction, the original loses some (if not all) of its aura. Loss of the aura also means that

anyone who comes in contact with the object being reproduced is free to interpret it in

---

[13] Throughout the first three seasons, the Council functions as the place of knowledge about Slayers and, as we find out in "Get It Done" (7.15), the Shadowmen, the first Watchers, actually created the Slayer by having a human woman breed with a supernatural entity – essentially giving us the birth of Christ.

[14] The hypocrisy of the believers is one of the top-cited issues most people say prevents them from attending a church.

whatever way they wish – everyone becomes a critic or expert on their own interpretation of

the work (Kolker 125). This is how we make Christ figures common as opposed to awe-

inspiring; by internalizing and personalizing this figure of sacrifice, we reproduce him in an

image we are comfortable with and feel capable of understanding. Campbell references this

as the Christ within, "the sense of mankind … in you" (*The Power of Myth* 263). Campbell

claims that in order to worship and live according to the word of whatever god we follow, we

must identify with that god (263). In order to do that, we make Christ common, human and

fallible, like us. These Common Christs do not take the place of Christ as savior, but because

we cannot identify with the perfect savior, they act as imitations of our attainable, preferred

view of Christ.

Hebrews 13:8 states that "Jesus Christ is the same yesterday and today and forever"

(NIV). For American Christianity and pop culture, however, this is far from true. Christ has

evolved from the prophesied Son of God to the historical man Jesus; from the sacrificial

lamb to the resurrected kerygmatic Christ; from his role as a traditional Christ figure to that

of a pop culture icon; until finally coming to the role of Common Christ. Now, as a Common

Christ, he is culturally inescapable – a representational savior for the masses who will fight to

save the world, but one who might join us for a drink after a hard day's work.

Chapter Two: *The X-Files* and Christ:

"The Truth is Out There"

Figure 1: Mulder as Christ in "The Sixth Extinction: Amor Fati" (7.2)[1]

Heralding the Common Christ

In the Gospels, John the Baptist heralds the coming of Christ the Messiah, the Truth. He is the "voice of one calling in the wilderness" who prepares the way for Jesus Christ's ministry. He prophesizes about the Messiah to come, baptizing people with water as a ritual cleansing of sin, but claims that another will come who will baptize with the Holy Spirit (John 1:34). When he sees Jesus, he proclaims him to be "the Lamb of God, who takes away the sin of the world!" (John 1:29).[2]

---

[1] *The X-Files.* Seventh Season DVD box set fold-out cover. Fox Broadcasting Company.

[2] The encounters with John and Jesus in the Gospels are found in Matthew 3:1-17, Mark 1:1-15, Luke 3:1-20 and John 1:1-34; John is also alluded to in a prophecy as the herald of Christ in Isaiah 40:3, saying one will come crying as a voice in the wilderness, as well as later in the Gospels when he is imprisoned and ultimately beheaded by Herod.

During its near decade-long run, *The X-Files* (1993-2002) served a role similar to that of John the Baptist in that it heralded a change not only in television programming but in the presentation of religion and Christ figures as well. Beginning four years before *Buffy* and ending three years before the start of *Supernatural, The X-Files* was an example of success for shows focused on the supernatural or paranormal that contained a Common Christ figure, and questioned the meaning of salvation and the function of religion in the American belief system.

For Paul Peterson, author of "Religion in *The X-Files*," the show provides one of the "deepest and most sophisticated treatments of religious phenomena ever found on network television" (181). While religious influences can be seen throughout the series in everything from the titles of certain episodes like "Eve" (1.11), "Lazarus" (1.15) "Born Again" (1.22), "Apocrypha" (3.16), and "Signs and Wonders" (7.9), to the golden cross Scully wears as a representation of her Catholic faith, to being a dominant force in specific episodes like "Revelations" (3.11) and "All Souls" (5.17), *The X-Files* is not a religious show.[3] *The X-Files* brought religion, science, mythology, American culture, the supernatural, and the paranormal all together to tell an overarching story of redemption and sacrifice in a way that made it not only an award-winning series during its initial run, but still inspires comparison, reviews and internet postings today, over ten years since the series finale.

The X-Files follows Special Agents Fox Mulder and Dana Scully as they probe cases that are unexplainable, or "x-files," to find the "truth" about what really happened. These cases may be biological, mystical, paranormal, supernatural or even extraterrestrial in nature.

---

[3] *The X-Files* did not just focus on Protestantism. "The Blessing Way" (3.1) featured Native American healing rituals, "Genderbender" (1.14) had an Amish sect, and "The Calusari" (2.21) focused on Romanian ritualistic faiths, just to name a few.

At its core, *The X-Files* tells us that "the truth is out there" if we just look for it hard enough. What that truth is, however, is different for everyone. Mulder searches for evidence of alien abductions and answers to what happened to his sister who disappeared from the family home when she was eight years old. For him, this seemingly supernatural answer is the truth in a world of lies and cover-ups. It is a truth that will help explain his loss and his grief, as well as justify his belief.

Scully, meanwhile, searches for the rational, scientific truth behind all the x-files she and Mulder investigate. She is the skeptic to Mulder's believer, even though she is a Catholic (sometimes she is more devout than other times, but her faith is ever present throughout the series). Many of the stand-alone episodes, those not part of the overarching storyline of the show (or mytharc, as it was called by fans), focus on Scully's Catholic faith and how she reconciles it with her devotion to medicine, science, and logic. An excellent example of this is the three-episode arc beginning with the Season 4 finale, "Gethsemane" (4.24) and continuing onto the two-part Season 5 premier episodes, "Redux" (5.1) and "Redux II" (5.2). While the mytharc is a driving force in these episodes, Scully is a main focus of the episode as she deals with terminal cancer.[4] In "Gethsemane," Scully turns away from her faith, saying that she is being treated by science instead. Over the course of the three episodes, however, we see her return to Catholicism after her cancer goes into remission. This pattern of distance and return to faith is one that happens over and over again for Scully as she never fully loses her position as skeptic.

---

[4] Though Scully eventually recovers from her cancer, I still call it terminal here because that is how it is referred to throughout these episodes. The doctors believe it to be terminal, as does Scully. The direness of this diagnosis is what prompts her return to Catholicism because it seems to be a miracle when she is healed.

Though Scully is the character with a professed religious affiliation, Mulder is the one classified as the staunch believer, the man of faith. The faith he has is not in God or organized religion, which he frequently dismisses as being silly at best and, in some cases, documented insanity at worst. His faith is in the "truth" that he searches for. Where Scully asks for evidence, Mulder trusts feelings, intuitions, and fringe sciences, such as hypnosis, telekinesis, and psychic phenomena. Our first introduction to him in the "Pilot" episode is a poster on a wall with a flying saucer with the text, "I Want to Believe." Throughout the series, Mulder displays a level of devotion to the x-files and to finding out the truth about his sister's disappearance that might be called religious in nature. He even speaks about his belief and search for truth in religious terminology. In "Colony" (2.16), Mulder explains, "I have lived with a fragile faith built on the ether of vague memories from an experience that I can neither prove nor explain. … To believe as passionately as I did was not without sacrifice, but I always accepted the risks." In this episode and the following one, "Endgame" (2.17), Mulder has found proof of alien life (though, of course, no hard evidence survives) and come in contact with aliens who claim to know what happened to his sister, that she is alive. Mulder feels vindicated in his life-long quest. As he battles to survive against an alien virus and hypothermia he says, "If I should die now, it would be with the certainty that my faith has been righteous. And if, through death, larger mysteries are revealed, I will have already learned the answer to the question that has driven me here" ("Colony"). Mulder's description of his revelation is not all that different from that of Christian saints and believers, giving his experience a decidedly religious tone.

"Colony" and "Endgame" are also moments when we see Mulder being portrayed as a Common Christ. In "Endgame," he meets a group of alien clones who are copies of his sister, Samantha. The clones establish Mulder as the one who can redeem his sister and save her:

> CLONE #1: She [Samantha] was the first one. The one from which we all came.The one you must save.
> MULDER: I'm not your savior.
> CLONE #4: You must help us. You have no choice.
> MULDER: No, I… I do have a choice and my choice is to walk out of here.

Mulder refuses to accept the position of savior at first. His refusal is easy to understand given the emotional stress he has been under concerning his sister. During the course of these two episodes, Mulder has gone from believing his sister returned, then believing she is dead, to finding out she was never here but replaced with an alien clone. One can sympathize with him for not wanting any extra responsibility. It is the second refusal that is interesting. The clones claim that he has no choice but to be the savior and Mulder says he does – he can leave. Ostensibly, Christ had a similar choice of whether or not to fulfill his role as savior, but that choice is never voiced. He expresses a desire to not go through with the suffering of salvation, but ultimately concedes. Traditional Christ figures also follow similar paths – they have a choice to avoid sacrifice, but always choose it. Mulder is given the ultimatum – it is his duty, his job to save the clones and his sister – and he opts to walk away. Though he later fulfills this savior role by chasing after the clones and the alien bounty hunter who is chasing them, he still maintains the separation from traditional Christ figures. As a Common Christ he does not attempt to save because it is his duty – he does it for a personal reason – finding the truth about his sister.

Mulder is seen as a Common Christ on several other occasions throughout the series, most notably in the "The Sixth Extinction: Amor Fati" (7.2), which was influenced by Nikos Kazantzakis' novel, *The Last Temptation of Christ*. David Duchovny, who portrayed Mulder and wrote "The Sixth Extinction," acknowledged that he saw many correlations between the struggles of Kazantzakis' Jesus, whom he found to be "profoundly human," and Mulder's own problems (Donaldson 4). Using this "very human model of Christ," Duchovny specifically stated that he was not trying to make Mulder into a "Christ-like savior figure, but rather an 'everyman'" (4). The episode openly acknowledges that Mulder is not a typical Christ when The Cigarette Smoking Man (CSM) tells him bluntly, "Only part of you is dying. The part that played the hero. You've suffered enough – for the X-Files, for your partner, for the world. You're not Christ."[5] A vision of Mulder's past informant, Deep Throat, tells Mulder that he is "not the hub of the universe, the cause of life and death." The whole episode is a vision quest for Mulder, who is in a coma, to decide his role as a savior. In Mulder's dreams, the CSM "tempts" Mulder (as Christ was tempted in the wilderness) with the promise of a new, normal, every-day life where he can settle down with a family. All Mulder has to do is choose to take it and reject his role as savior.

As the CSM arranges for Mulder to be operated on in reality, he tells an ally not to feel sorry for Mulder: "Don't think of the man… Think of the sacrifice he's making for all of us… for the world." Once again, Mulder is cast as a traditional Christ figure, but he is not willingly sacrificing himself here, as the woman points out when she says, "It would've been nice to give him a choice" on whether or not to go through with the procedure. In the end, Mulder gives himself the choice – not on whether to have the operation, but whether or not to give up and stop fighting. As with "Colony" and "Endgame," Mulder is not moved to action

---

[5] And yet the Christological imagery and references continue, even to the point of having Mulder "crucified" on a medical table, arms and legs extended as if on a cross with a crown of thorns (a surgical strap and equipment) about his head (Donaldson 7). Ironically, during this scene, despite having told Mulder he is not Christ, the CSM identifies him as his "savior" because Mulder exists as an alien-human hybrid, something CSM's group has been attempting to achieve for many years.

by the plight of the world, but by the love and motivation from Scully. He dreams of Scully, of her faith and trust in him, and wakes up, resurrected from his dying body in the dream to a new life and a new resolve to "fight the fight."

This same sense of resolve is a repeat of what Mulder experiences at the end of the double episode arc of "Colony" and "Endgame." Though Mulder does not find the answers he hoped for, he has found something else: "I found something I thought I'd lost. Faith to keep looking." Throughout the series, Mulder keeps his faith without fail, regardless of the lack of hard evidence that he has of his beliefs.[6] Scully, meanwhile, is as skeptical as ever, even after all she sees and experiences. She acknowledges that the cases might be explainable if we accept the "possibility of paranormal phenomena," but is "convinced that to accept such conclusions is to abandon all hope of understanding the scientific events behind them" ("Endgame"). Even though she does confess that her experiences have "challenged [her] faith and [her] belief in an ordered universe" she states that "this uncertainty has only strengthened [her] need to know, to understand, to apply reason to those things which seem to defy it" ("Endgame"). By "The Sixth Extinction," however, Scully's skepticism has a different tone. She is still disbelieving, but she does not have the same conviction:

> SCULLY: Mulder, I don't believe that. I... I don't believe it. It's impossible.
> MULDER: Is it any more impossible than what you saw in Africa or what you
> saw in me? *(referencing a flying saucer and alien biology)*
> SCULLY: I don't know what to believe anymore. ... I don't even know... I
> don't know... I don't know what the truth is... I don't know who
> to listen to. I don't know who to trust.

---

[6] There is a brief period at the beginning of Season 5 beginning with "Redux" and "Redux II" when Mulder doubts the existence of extraterrestrials. For about half the season, Mulder's faith waivers as he tries to decipher the truth of The Smoking Man's allegations that instead of the government suppressing the truth about aliens, they have been hiding their activities under the guise of alien abductions and sightings. Finally in "The Red and the Black," (5.14), Mulder's faith is restored after witnessing various phenomena.

This is quite a radical shift for Scully. She is trying desperately to hold on to her skepticism because it is a safe space for her, a comfort zone. For the majority of the series, Scully has relied upon the scientific method, data and science to support her theories; but here, she is lost without it (Davis et al 195). Science has failed to help her explain the alien craft she has seen and what Mulder has experienced, but unlike "Endgame," she does not find a renewed vow to look deeper for more answers. She is unable to fully accept what happened as truth simply because it does not match up to her vision of what truth should be, and yet at the end of the episode she finds a truth she can live with in Mulder's acceptance and companionship.

In "Beyond the Sea" (1.12), "Revelations" (3.11), and "All Souls" (5.17) we see a reverse of this relationship in that Mulder becomes the skeptic and Scully the believer.[7] In these three episodes, the supernatural phenomena is true, but Mulder refuses to believe in it because of his own blindness to what the truth should look like. In "Beyond the Sea," Mulder does not want to imagine someone like Luther Boggs, a psychopathic murderer, as having the type of psychic ability he believes in. Mulder admits this, saying "I believe in psychic ability, without a doubt, but not in this case. Not Boggs." The reason Scully begins to believe is because she is having visions of her father who dies suddenly at the beginning of the episode, trying to speak to her, including one in which Boggs begins singing the song playing at his funeral and calls her by her father's pet name for her, "Starbuck." When she follows clues from Boggs' psychic vision to discover a crime scene, Mulder is furious that she believed Boggs. Mulder says her lack of skepticism is because of her emotional state. Her grief over the death of her father is "clouding [her] judgment" and putting herself in danger. The irony

---

[7] In "Beyond the Sea," we have another moment of Christ imagery with Mulder. Boggs warns him not to "go near the white cross. We see you down... and your blood spills on the white cross." Later, while chasing the suspect, Mulder is shot near a leaning pile of lumber. When Scully reaches him, she sees that two white boards are leaned in such a way to form a cross and Mulder's blood from the gunshot wound is sprayed across it.

is that Mulder himself is often emotionally and personally invested in his work with the x-files because of the loss of his sister. Mulder's desire to find answers about his sister's disappearance often clouds his judgment and causes him to risk life and career. In the case of Boggs, Mulder urges her to be open to "extreme possibilities only when they're the truth." Ironically, Boggs' abilities are truth – just not the truth that Mulder wishes to see.

Since "Beyond the Sea" is so early on in the series, it only makes sense that Scully is not completely without her skepticism at the end. Even after following Boggs' leads and seeing visions of her dead father, Scully still tries to explain it away rationally, finally admitting to Mulder when he questions her that she is "afraid to believe" in it all. By the time of "Revelations" in Season 3, however, Scully has experienced more, making her skepticism harder to hold on to. Being skeptical is even more difficult in this case because the phenomenon being explored is religious in nature. She finds herself conflicted between having faith that the boy they are investigating is actually displaying signs of the stigmata and wanting to find an alternate, non-faith based explanation. There is no real conflict for Mulder because he automatically rejects the religious "miracle" of a boy displaying the stigmata as being real. As already stated, Mulder views anything religious as being nonsense.

Perhaps "anything religious" is a bit of a stretch. After all, he does go along with Native American religious beliefs in "Shapes" (1.18) and Romanian ritualistic faith in "The Calusari" (2.21). More specifically, Mulder has issues with anything Protestant. In "Revelations," he flat out dismisses the bible as being nothing more than a "parable, a metaphor for the truth, not the truth itself" and calls the stories of saints and religious miracles "hagiographic fabrications, not historical truths." He has no problems believing in aliens, ghosts, werewolves, mutant humans who can stretch their bodies, live without aging and require human livers to stay young forever, but when God and Christianity enter as the possible explanation, Mulder requires enormous amounts of proof.

When Scully admits that she believes God creates miracles, Mulder asks if her belief continues "even if science can't explain them," to which Scully replies, "maybe that's just what faith is" ("Revelations"). Scully even calls him out on this double-standard of requiring proof, using a parody of the lines he so often gives her when she is skeptical of something she has just witnessed: "You go out on a limb whenever you see a light in the sky, but you're unwilling to accept the possibility of a miracle, even when it's right in front of you?" ("Revelations"). And here is a difference worth noting between Scully's and Mulder's skepticism. Scully tries to find logical, realistic solutions, but she is not above allowing herself to believe in the light of overwhelming evidence. Mulder, however, who is usually so open-minded about possible extraterrestrial phenomena, refuses to believe in a Christian answer. Zack Handlen, a contributing writer to *The A.V. Club*, an online review and entertainment newspaper, argues that Mulder refuses to accept a Christian answer because to do so would alter the world from the way he needs it to be.[8]

Handlen understands why Mulder has issues with the idea of Christian faith being the answer to the types of x-files usually seen on the show. To say that Christ exists, that there is a God, requires a "massive overhaul of one's notion of existence" because having proof that there's a Christian God would seem to disregard all the other phenomena that Mulder and Scully encounter in the show (Handlen). The only way to have God be an answer would be to have him exist on the same level as all the other aliens and monsters the show has examined,

---

[8] *The A.V. Club* is published by the satirical faux news publication, *The Onion*, but *The A.V. Club* is not like its parent. It publishes legitimate reviews, interviews and articles on various modes of the entertainment industry ranging from music to television shows to video game culture.

which would effectively make him not God in terms of the Christian faith (Handlen). Instead of being the one, true, "thou shalt have no other gods before me" God, he would simply be an equal force amongst the many.

At the end of "Revelations," Scully visits a priest and asks if he believes in miracles, the kind of events that "defy explanation." She specifically says she is talking to him because she cannot approach Mulder with this discussion. She knows he would mock her or dismiss her instead of listening. When she expresses doubt about what she's witnessed, it is Mulder's skepticism that makes her question:

> PRIEST: Why do you doubt yourself?
> SCULLY: Because my partner didn't see them. He didn't… he didn't believe
> them. And usually he… he believes without question.

Scully doubts the truth of her experience and her role as protector and savior – one that she was at first hesitant to accept – because they force her to question not only the world of science and logic, but also her own faith. In this episode more than any other at the time, Scully reveals her Catholic upbringing, reciting stories of saints she learned in the catechism and relating elements of the case to religious doctrine. Usually, she is the one who does not believe, even when she *has* seen actual, supernatural phenomena, but in this case the roles of sceptic are reversed. Mulder does not see, does not believe, in essence, does not trust in Scully's belief; this is something he asks her to do all the time – to trust him, even if she does not believe. But here, because Scully has faith and believes in a religious explanation, Mulder's response to her makes her doubt herself and her faith. Having faith in the truth of the universe is not the same as having faith in the Truth.

This disregard for organized religion and the conflict of personal faith is a strong theme once again in "All Souls" (5.17). In this episode, Scully tries to understand a case of ritualistic murder – two sisters, part of quadruplets, are found dead with their eyes burnt out and their bodies in a position of prayer. When she begins to voice religious theories, Mulder shuts her down. Even when she tries to couch it in language he might respect, calling it "supernatural" instead of religious, Mulder says, "Religion has masqueraded as the paranormal since the dawn of time to justify some of the most horrible acts in history" ("All Souls"). He once again tells Scully to be careful of letting her personal issues and beliefs cloud her judgment. Mulder's refusal to see anything but his own version of the truth is in full force here.

Part of the issue with Mulder's refusal to, at least, be open to the possibility of a religious explanation is that his rejection of any reality but his own is dangerous. Just as he explains so often to Scully that keeping an open mind will keep her alive, his rejection of any truth but his own can endanger people. In both cases, forces beyond the normal realm of reality are being invoked; the only difference is that Mulder's view does not come with a constrictive rule book and origin story – the Bible. A priest who is trying to save the remaining girls' lives tells him "your secular prejudices blind you from seeing what's really happening here. … Unless you accept the truth of God's teachings … you are but fools rushing in! You put your own lives in danger as well as the lives of the messengers" ("Revelations"). This is the same type of warning to accept the truth that Mulder uses on Scully time and time again. It also appears in *Buffy* and *Supernatural*, where a refusal to believe in the existence of some supernatural force, religious or not, has the possibility of resulting in bodily harm or death.[9]

---

[9] In *Supernatural* especially, we see this dichotomy of belief and skepticism play out between Sam and Dean over religious matters, most notably in "Faith" (1.12) and "Houses of the Holy" (2.13). A new discussion of religion then begins from Season 4 onward as the existence of God, angels, Lucifer and other biblical themes becomes part of the show's canon.

A separate layer of skepticism and religious discussion exists in "All Souls" that is not present in "Beyond the Sea" or "Revelations," and that is the attitude of the Church towards Scully's experiences. In "All Souls," Scully sees a vision of a man who appears to have the face of a lion, an eagle and a bull before he disappears in a bright light. When she asks a priest about it, he tells her of the legend of angels that look like this, the Seraphim – angels who mate with human women and produce four offspring which they then return to Earth to collect. The legend of the Seraphim matches the details of the case almost exactly. Scully asks if that is what she saw and the priest says, "No, what you saw was a figment of your imagination. A half-remembered story from your childhood that has surfaced because of this case." When Scully insists it was real, the priest says the book the legend comes from is not even canonical; "the text in which it appears isn't even recognized by the Church." Once again, Scully, the skeptic, shows belief when those who should be the first to profess similar belief are failing to do so, but this time it is not Mulder and his rejection of religion in the way – it is a member of the Church. The priest shares her faith, so he should be one of the first to support her theories, yet he does not. But when she asks if he believes God has a plan, he immediately affirms that he does. He has the faith of the organization – everything within the canon is fine – but when something happens that might pull him beyond that, beyond his realm of what he believes to be true, he backs away, just as Mulder does.

Whether it is a lack of belief on Mulder's part or the Church's, the relationship of truth, religion, and personal faith within the show is important. Though most of the episodes that focus on religion are stand-alone episodes not directly connected to the mytharc, an overarching theme pervades the episodes that have religion at the heart of their stories (Peterson 194). It is not that the show presents faith as being wrong or false; if it did, then each of the cases involving religion would turn out to have a secondary, traditionally

supernatural explanation. Instead, we get a truth that no character in the show but Scully is

privy to that is being shared with the audience. That is not entirely accurate – the truth is

made available to other characters within the show, most often Mulder himself – but Scully is

the only one to believe it.

This should cause others to share her belief – or at least consider it plausible –

because everything about Scully should result in her being taken seriously. Her intelligence,

her seriousness, her professionalism, her scientific background all establish her as a character

who does not run off to flights of fancy (Peterson 195). It is a running joke amongst fans of

the series about her ability to be skeptical of things, despite all she has experienced with

Mulder. In fact, Mulder asks her that same question – "After all you've seen, after all the

evidence, why can't you believe?" ("Beyond the Sea" 1.12). It is a theme of the show, and

yet when Scully does believe, when she is moved beyond her skepticism, no one believes

with her.[10] They feel that the previous existence of her Catholic faith makes her less credible

as a judge of the truth. Even members of the Church who share the same upbringing and

would normally counsel her not to get so wrapped up in her world of science and logic, tell

her that such belief is merely her imagination. In this, Scully becomes a quintessential

Common Christ. She is separate from the tradition of belief; she is rejected by the existent

faith and those closest to her (much like Christ was rejected by the Pharisees and Peter); and

---

[10] When filming "The Sixth Extinction," Gillian Anderson (the actress who plays Scully) felt Scully's level of
skepticism was bizarre after all this time, especially in this episode considering how the previous episode had
seen Scully encountering a space ship. Series creator Chris Carter told her that the show needed the believer vs
skeptic dynamic in order to function, so they continued to have her be skeptical, despite all she experienced
(Hurwitz and Knowles 174).

she works to save the world not out of a devotion to the Church, but out of a sense of personal conviction and desire to make things right.

The Truth is Out There

For the majority of its nine seasons, *The X-Files* is a search for "the truth" and an attempt to reveal conspiracies and government cover-ups. This truth ranges from the existence of alien life, to life after death, to the reality of evolution, and even to the reality of God. In all but a handful of episodes, the intro sequence ends with the tagline, "The Truth Is Out There."[11] Mulder believes this – that the truth is out there – and that the truth will provide closure, peace, or understanding. It will bring, to a certain extent, salvation and possibly forgiveness – as long as it is his version of truth. In this tagline, we hear an echo of one of the basic tenets of Christianity, which is Christ's proclamation that he is "the way, the truth and the life. No one comes to the Father except through me" (John 14:6). But if Christ is "the truth," the one and only, and not just "a truth," then the Christian church is seen as having a monopoly on the representation and presentation of salvation. It is fulfilling the same role of the government in *The X-Files* – they regulate who does or does not receive salvation by controlling "the truth."

In "Fallen Angel" (1.10), an episode which almost sees Mulder booted from the FBI and the x-files division closed for good, Mulder must go before a review board to discuss the case of a missing man whom Mulder believes was abducted. Throughout the review, the board members constantly shut Mulder's evidence down, claiming to be in possession of the

---

[11] Out of the series' 202 episodes, only 19 ran a different tag line than "The Truth is Out There," with some of these echoing the same sentiment such as one written in Navajo that translates to "The truth is far from here" ("Anasazi" 2.25) or one in German, "Die Wahrheit ist Irgendwo da drauben" – "the truth is out there somewhere" ("Triangle" 6.3). In the final season, we also get "erehT tuO si hturT ehT," which is "The Truth is Out There," backwards ("4-D" 9.4).

truth about what really happened. As he is leaving, Mulder shouts at them, "no one … has

jurisdiction over the truth." When examined in conjunction with the show's attitude towards

religion, one cannot help but note the similarities, and the irony. Mulder is in constant search

of the truth, which he feels is being withheld from him, but he often displays a certain

authority in terms of deciding what is and what is not the truth. In his article "The Strange

Discourse of *The X-Files*: What It Is, What It Does, and What Is at Stake," Joe Bellon argues

that *The X-Files* is both subversive and liberating. It teaches us not to "rely on blind faith in

government or science … [but] … on our own abilities to judge external truths and discover

internal truths" (152). But what those truths are in terms of religious beliefs is harder to

figure out.

Chapter Three: *Buffy, the Vampire Slayer* –

Just a Girl: The Savior in a Micro-Mini

Figure 2: Buffy's sacrificial leap at the end of "The Gift" (5.22)[1]

A year before *The X-Files* aired in 1993, American film audiences were introduced to a blonde teenager from the Valley named Buffy who, apart from being an airhead and a cheerleader, also turned out to be the one destined to fight the forces of darkness. She was "the Vampire Slayer." The film achieved mild success for blending the genres of teen comedy and horror, and although it was never a breakout hit with audiences at the theaters, it did become a cult hit not long after being released on video and DVD. Five years later in 1997, Buffy Summers, still the Slayer but not nearly as airheaded, transferred to the small screen into Sunnydale High School to battle demons, vampires, monsters and a whole slew of social issues for seven seasons, as well as sparking a spinoff show, *Angel*.[2] Apart from the shared title of *Buffy, the Vampire Slayer*, however, the two works were almost completely different.

---

[1] Screen capture provided by BuffyWorld.Com.
[2] These two shows are known collectively as the "Buffyverse."

Joss Whedon, creator and writer of both the movie and the series, has said that his original vision for Buffy was meant to subvert the horror genre by having the "little blonde girl who goes into a dark alley and gets killed, in every horror movie" turn out to be the hero rather than the victim.[3] While both versions of *Buffy* still have this subversion, the film was turned into a campy, cultish comedy that focused on the absurdity of a cheerleader named Buffy – teamed up with the young drifter Pike – fighting the leather-clad, cape-wearing undead. The film was nowhere near as dark and issue-driven as Whedon had originally intended it to be, which is partly why he later chose to craft the story as a television series under his own direction and control. The success and reception of shows like *The Simpsons*, *Xena: Warrior Princess*, and *The X-Files* also helped in terms of getting production backing because they showed that American audiences were interested in strong female leads, dark comedy, and the paranormal.

Buffy on television was much truer to the original scope of Whedon's idea about a monster-slaying teenage girl. And she had more help than a single, young drifter. Buffy's support system (affectionately called the Scoobies both in and outside the show as a reference to the original gang of teenaged-mystery solvers on *Scooby Doo*) included her friends Xander, Willow, Cordelia and Oz; her Watcher, Giles; her vampire lovers, Angel and Spike; ex-vengeance demon, Anya; paramilitary demon-hunter boyfriend, Riley; and sister, Dawn, as well as a smaller supporting cast of Potential Slayers and acquaintances. If that list seems a bit strange, it is because of the types of situations that happen on *Buffy* – this show is not the typical high school teen drama. In the Buffyverse, "the problems teenagers face become literal monsters" (Wilcox, *Why Buffy Matters* 178). Together, Buffy and the

---

[3] Audio Commentary. "Welcome to the Hellmouth." *Buffy, the Vampire Slayer*. Dir. Joss Whedon. 1997. 20th Century Fox, 2002. DVD.

Scoobies face down demons and the treacherous waters of dating; they battle monsters and

the trauma of boring classes and pop quizzes; they contend with vampires and the parental

pressure to succeed. Each of these issues carries the same weight. This is part of what makes

Buffy stand out from other supernatural-based programming. Instead of putting the everyday,

mundane situations of life as a low priority against the supernatural fiends and elements,

Buffy constantly sets them side by side with preventing the apocalypse and stopping the

forces of evil.

This combination of the everyday and the supernatural also means that the intricacies

and relationships on the show, as well as the mythology of the show itself, are fairly difficult

to follow at times. Instead of the writers dumbing the show down, the audience is expected to

pay closer attention, to become involved, so that conversations like the following from the

final season not only make sense, but are entertaining because we understand that the show is

poking fun at its own twisted mythology:

> GILES: Uh, it's a long story.
> BUFFY: The military put a chip in Spike's head so he couldn't hurt anyone.
> GILES: And that would be the abridged version.
> BUFFY: But he wouldn't hurt anyone anymore because he has a soul now.
> GILES: Unless the First triggers him again.
> ROBIN: Triggers the chip?
> BUFFY: No, the trigger's a post-hypnotic thing. The First put it in his head. …
> He was killing again.
> ROBIN: So, he has a trigger, a soul, and a chip?
> GILES: Not anymore.
> BUFFY: It was killing him, Giles.
> ROBIN: The trigger?
> BUFFY: No, the chip. The trigger's not active anymore.
> ROBIN: Because the military gave him a soul? (*Buffy and Giles glare at Robin, who throws up his hands*) Sorry.[4]

---

[4] "Lies My Parents Told Me" (7.17). All dialogue is taken from the episode transcripts collected at BuffyWorld.com.

Whedon expected greater focus and involvement from his audience on the most basic

storyline level (Wilcox *Why Buffy Matters* 178). Aside from merely remembering character

relationship histories, demonic mythologies, and story continuities from season to season,

audiences needed to be able to discern the underlying metaphors and symbols within the

show.

For the first few seasons, these metaphors are fairly straightforward. In "The Witch"

(1.3), for example, the storyline centers on a mother who uses witchcraft to swap bodies with

her teenage daughter. This is reminiscent of the idea of parents trying to live vicariously

through their children. Another early example is "The Pack" (1.6), in which Xander is

possessed by a feral animal spirit, which causes a radical behavioral change. When Buffy

tries to explain this change to Giles, her watcher has a more practical reason for it:

> GILES: Xander's taken to teasing the less fortunate?
> BUFFY: Uh-huh.
> GILES: And, there's been a noticeable change in both clothing and demeanor?
> BUFFY: Yes.
> GILES: And, well, otherwise all his spare time is spent lounging about with
> imbeciles?
> BUFFY: It's bad, isn't it?
> GILES: It's devastating. He's turned into a sixteen-year-old boy. Of course,
> you'll have to kill him.
> BUFFY: Giles, I'm serious.
> GILES: So am I. Except for the part about killing him. Testosterone is a great
> equalizer. It turns all men into morons. He will, however, get over it.

Giles all but announces that the animal possession storyline is a metaphor for puberty. As the

series progresses, these metaphors get denser and more emotionally suggestive. Instead of

stand-alone episode metaphors, there became season-long arcs, as is evident in Seasons 6 and

7.

Season 6 of *Buffy* sees Buffy dead and resurrected, trying (and failing) to go back to

college, holding down a low-end McJob to make ends meet, and trying to be a parent to her sister, Dawn.[5] While all this happens, she also has to contend with the loss of a father figure

as Giles goes back to England, the depression at being ripped out of Heaven that has pushed

her into an emotionally unhealthy relationship with Spike, and a general sense of apathy

about life. These issues are explored through episodes like "Gone," in which Buffy turns

invisible – a physical manifestation of how she has felt ever since her resurrection. This

season is less about the supernatural evil and more about the harshness of human reality. The

Big Bad for the majority of the season is a trio of nerds who are more annoyances than any

real danger, leaving Buffy and the Scoobies to face the terrifying nature of life after high

school/college. Season 6 also explores drug addiction and relapse through the metaphor of

Willow's addiction to magic.

In Season 7, *Buffy* looks at the notions of self-doubt and leadership. Buffy must take a

group of Potential Slayers and turn them into a full fighting force, but she is not certain that

she is a good leader. Adding to her doubt is the Big Bad of the season, The First (as in, The

First Evil). The First can take on the shape and personality of anyone who has died, which in

the case of *Buffy* opens the doors for several characters to come back. Buffy has to listen to

doubt and criticism of her skills and abilities not only from her friends and the Potentials, but

also from herself, literally. She has died, therefore The First can take her form – it looks just

like her and speaks with her voice. Buffy must overcome being taunted by her failures – the

voices of those she could not save – as well as her own inner-doubts in order to defeat The

First.

Out of all the metaphors and symbols that Whedon employs in the Buffyverse,

however, none are so strongly contested and discussed as the religious ones, especially those

---

[5] Buffy and Dawn's mother, Joyce, died of an aneurysm in the Season 5 episode, "The Body" (5.16). After her
mother's death, Buffy was granted guardianship of Dawn and took over the role as caretaker for her.

that are Christian in nature. Part of this controversy stems from the fact that Whedon is a

professed atheist, so some find it difficult to believe that he would deliberately put Christian

symbolism into his work.[6] Taking into account Ziolkowski's discussion of the Gospels as a

cultural property now rather than merely a religious one, however, I would argue that a

Christian reading of *Buffy* is entirely possible. A large portion of the Buffyverse is based in

Christian mythology. Some of the religious symbols are obvious. Buffy uses crosses and holy

water to repel vampires, and upside-down crucifixes to revoke vampire access to homes.

Aside from vampires, she also fights demons and visits hell-dimensions. In fact, Sunnydale,

California, the town which *Buffy* is set in, is situated on top of a Hellmouth, a portal to a hell

dimension. There is also talk of heaven and miracles, such as the unusual snowfall in

"Amends" (3.10) which prevents Angel's suicide-by-sunrise, or Buffy's description in

"Afterlife" (6.3) of where she went after sacrificing her life at the end of Season 5 as being

someplace where she was "warm … loved … finished." She says, "I don't understand about

theology or dimensions, or any of it, really, but I think I was in heaven."[7]

The critics who discuss religion in *Buffy* spend so much time trying to argue whether

Buffy does or does not have a religious dimension that, with a few exceptions, they usually

fail to notice what happens when a religious lens is applied to the show. In his article, "No

Big Win: Themes of Sacrifice, Salvation, and Redemption," Gregory Sakal argues that *Buffy*

---

[6] This same argument about the presence of religion is applicable to any number of Whedon properties. The center debate of *Dollhouse* is whether it is ok for people to play God and the location of the soul inside mankind. *Marvel's Agents of S.H.I.E.L.D.* looks at the presence of God and science in the evolution of mankind. *Angel* focuses on the redemption of personal sins. *Firefly* actually has a religious leader – a "shepherd" – on the ship, which brings in any number of religious storylines. *Buffy* is just the first.

[7] Wendy Love Anderson's "Prophecy Girl and The Powers that Be: The Philosophy of Religion in the Buffyverse" has a more thorough discussion of the fan response and questioning of the religious symbolism of the snowfall in "Amends," as well as Whedon's own response to it. Anderson also points out that Buffy's "heaven" is later paralleled in Season 6 as being a "delusional, demon-induced world in which Buffy is a psychiatric patient" (218).

is not religious in any way, especially not Christian, claiming that "despite a few arguably Christian overtones," such as vampires fearing crosses and holy water, for example, a religious overlay of the show is not really possible (239). Wendy Love Anderson, in "Prophecy Girl and the Powers that Be: The Philosophy of Religion in the Buffyverse," explains that the world of *Buffy* is not so easily secularized. Not even considering the use of crosses and holy water as symbols of religious power and rightness against the wrongness of demons and vampires, Anderson cites the routine encounters that Buffy and the Scoobies have with cults, gods and manifestations of their power, religious artifacts and prophetic writings (213-214). What Anderson finds interesting is that, in the Buffyverse, religion is frequently "*demonized,* in both the literal and figurative sense of the term" (author's emphasis, 214). Whenever Buffy and the Scoobies encounter an identifiably religious group or person, they almost always turn out to be involved in something evil, or at the very least, not beneficial to humanity.

Buffy seldom relies upon traditionally religious models to confront this evil, however. Even when she does use religious objects, knowledge or texts, what is more important is the bonds of Buffy and her friends, not the item's religious nature (Anderson 217). She and the Scoobies may use rituals or invoke magic in order to combat their foes, but these forces are almost always referenced in terms of the individual using it instead of as a petition to a god or religious force. The power of the magic, ritual or relic depends upon the person wielding it, not the nature of the object itself. Whenever there is a suggestion that the power comes from an outside authority, the idea is presented in a negative light. For instance, when Willow's magic use in Seasons 6 and 7 becomes dangerous, the magic suddenly becomes connected to specific beings or entities instead of the vague "spirits" it had been tied to before.

At the end of the series, when Willow uses magic to unlock the Slayer power in all women, there is no specific incantation. Once again, magic becomes secondary and Willow is the central focus – this is no longer a religious-based ritual, and therefore, not dangerous or demonized. So even though Anderson claims the Buffyverse is more sacred than Sakal would agree, she still agrees that "religion is not necessary" in this world for Buffy to be successful (217). In her article, "'She Believes in Me': Angel, Spike and Redemption," Melanie Wilson agrees more with Anderson in that the Buffyverse has a religious sense to it, especially with the use of mystical forces or "The Powers That Be,"[8] but she also pulls from Sakal's point of view in saying that though the show shares common themes with Christianity, it cannot be categorized as "strictly Christian" (137).

One of the few works that examines *Buffy* with the presumption of the show having a religious overlay is Jana Riess' *What Would Buffy Do? The Vampire Slayer as Spiritual Guide*. Unlike Sakal and Wilson, Riess has no problems identifying *Buffy* as a work teeming with religious symbolism and values, specifically those of Christianity. Riess identifies the function of *Buffy* as being similar to a medieval morality play (xi). As seen in texts such as *Everyman* or *Pilgrim's Progress,* character names in *Buffy* offer some interesting considerations: Angel is obvious, as is Faith, and Will, which is Willow's nickname. The characters and show may or may not personally have relationships with a Christian God or make direct mentions of Him or Christianity, but Riess argues that their actions and values are directly related to a Christian influence, representing a "secular universe saturated with

---

[8] "The Powers That Be," or TPTB, exist in the Buffyverse canon but were mainly used on the spinoff *Angel*. They were mentioned on *Buffy* once in "Becoming, Parts I and II" (2.21-22).

grace" (xi-xii). Riess sets Buffy and other characters up as traditional Christ figures of sacrifice, forgiveness and salvation, and if not spiritual, at least social redemption.

It is fairly easy to see Buffy in the role of the Christ figure, the one and only "way, the truth and the life." In a voice-over intro sequence for the first season, and several times throughout the show's run, Buffy is described as "the Chosen One. She alone will stand against the vampires, the demons and the forces of darkness. She is the Slayer." Even when the mythology of the show is changed and more than one Slayer comes into existence at a time, Buffy is still referred to as *the* Slayer. She is set up as something special, above. She is told by a Spirit Guide that "death is [her] gift" ("Intervention" 5.18), a gift she uses to sacrifice herself for her sister, friends and, ultimately, the world. When it is time to save the world at the end of the fifth season, only Buffy can be the sacrifice because her blood is what can close the portal, a reference to the power of being "washed in the blood" of Christ. When she jumps into the portal, she assumes a crucified position, with arms outstretched and, like Christ, she is later resurrected from the grave.

For Riess, Buffy is responsible for the salvation of the world, if not spiritually, then at least physically. Though Buffy saves the world from being sucked into a hell dimension or torn apart by demons, she does not "save" the people of the world in the Christian sense of the salvation of the soul; "Christ atoned for people's sins, but on *Buffy*, people must atone for their own" (Riess 119). Neither Buffy, nor any of the other characters who function in terms of sacrifice within the Buffyverse, can fully redeem people. Instead, *Buffy* explains that society is responsible for its own personal salvation, and that will not come easily. As Riess says, "redemption is hard work, and it is up to us" (120). This is partially why I argue that *Buffy* works as an example of the Common Christ phenomenon.

Buffy is a Common Christ rather than a Christ figure. She is not some strange, inexplicable, unattainable sacrifice; she is a teenage girl. She is the Slayer, a supernatural being, but one whose evolution is explainable. The Watchers have centuries of records and lore about her and her powers. The source of her power is known. When she is resurrected from the dead, it is through magical means, but every step of the spell is explained and understood as a work of human effort, not the intervention of some mystical deity. Buffy is human and embraces her humanity; she does not want to stand out from the crowd. When she rescues a young man in "The Gift" (5.22), he expresses disbelief at her abilities, saying "you're just a girl," and Buffy replies, "That's what I keep saying." She is not a figure of perfection that we can never hope to pay back for saving us. All she asks in return for her sacrifice in "The Gift" is for us to "live."

Buffy also functions as a Common Christ because she does not sacrifice herself simply for the betterment of all mankind or because it is her destiny. In the finale of Season 1, a prophecy is found that claims Buffy will die fighting The Master, a powerful vampire and the main villain of Season 1. When she hears this prophecy, she refuses to go, even though not doing so could have dire consequences for Sunnydale, if not the world. She tells Giles, "I quit! I resign ... I don't care! I don't care. Giles, I'm sixteen years old. I don't wanna die" ("Prophecy Girl" 1.12). Even though she has willingly accepted her position as the Slayer on other occasions, when it becomes an issue of her death versus saving the world, she is not willing to sacrifice herself. Her mind is changed, however, after her friend witnesses a scene of violence and death, the type of scene that will happen all too often should the Master rise. Buffy fights to save the world specifically *for* her friends and family to continue living in it; she does not sacrifice herself for strangers.

This theme of selfish salvation continues throughout the series. In Season 5, Buffy refuses to accept a plan that requires her to kill Dawn to stop the "unbearable torment and death" of "every living creature in this and every other dimension" ("The Gift"). In fact, she even threatens to kill any of her friends who try to kill Dawn to stop the apocalypse. Buffy understands that she is going against her calling as the Slayer to protect the world. She's sacrificed before – killing Angel to seal a portal at the end of Season 2, for example – but now she says, "I knew what was right. I don't have that anymore. I don't understand. I don't know how to live in this world if these are the choices. If everything just gets stripped away. I don't see the point" ("The Gift"). Questioning her role does not prevent her from being a Christ figure – even Christ questioned his role in the Garden of Gethsemane, praying, "Father, if You are willing, remove this cup from Me; yet not My will, but Yours be done" (Luke 22:42). Buffy becomes a Common Christ because she does not follow the "yet not my will" aspect of sacrifice. Instead, she tells Giles that if Dawn has to die, "I'm done with it. I'm quitting" ("The Gift").

In the end, quitting is not the choice Buffy makes. She sacrifices herself in Dawn's place. But instead of that being her final action, Buffy is resurrected through magic to continue the fight. This is another aspect of her status as a Common Christ. Instead of a Christ figure whose sacrifice satisfies a debt once and for all, Buffy and the Scoobies must give continually. This is similar to the parable of the servants waiting for the master's return in Luke 12:48: "From everyone to whom much has been given, much will be required; and from the one to whom much has been entrusted, even more will be demanded." Buffy has been entrusted with the world, so it is no surprise that what is demanded of her often has impact on a global scale. If she were a traditional Christ figure, her death would be all that was required – after all, we cannot ask much more from a person than to die. And yet, she is called back.

Riess thus concludes that "the Buffyverse contains no external savior whose act wipes the slate clean" for everyone once and for all (119). There is always another vampire to be staked, another demon to be vanquished, and another apocalypse to be thwarted. Early in the series, Buffy laments this fact, saying that her work is "fruitless:" "No fruit for Buffy," she says sadly, asking "is Sunnydale any better than when I first came here? Okay, so I battle evil. But I don't really win. The bad keeps coming back and getting stronger" ("Gingerbread" 3.11).

This realization does not stop Buffy from fighting, but it does point out an absence of the type of Christ/salvation figure we expect. Out of all the sacrifices made on *Buffy*, from small things like missing out on a "normal" life to dying, not one of them is ever good enough to stop the need for sacrifice ever again. And none of them completely wipe away all sin and guilt. After a rocky Season 6 where Willow tries to destroy the world she says, "It's nice to be forgiven. Too bad I need so much of it" ("Same Time, Same Place" 7.3). Where Christianity proposes one savior and one forgiveness for all and every sin, the Common Christ format of *Buffy* makes us responsible for our own forgiveness and redemption. There is no one-and-done savior in *Buffy*, and by the end of the series, there is not even a singular Christ figure. Instead, with the awakening of all the Potentials into actual Slayers, and the idea that all women everywhere who could be Slayers, now have that power, we have a world full of saving figures. The finale of the series is one of hope and salvation. The world is saved and the Hellmouth closed for good, but instead of a new heaven and a new earth as Revelation promises, we have a new order of salvation – a new shared power of Slayers.

While there is no end of examples that could be brought up to examine how Buffy and the core group of characters in the show exemplify the premise of Common Christs – what I have offered merely scratches the surface – there are two main themes within *Buffy* that illustrate it: forgiveness and patriarchal power structures. These two elements are traditionally tied to the Church, with the power lying in the ability to control knowledge, forgiveness, and salvation. In *Buffy*, we question that power by offering a model of distributed power and knowledge and taking responsibility for our own salvation.

Forgive, and Ye Shall Be Forgiven[9]

In *Buffy*, the characters often do more than simply tell a story. They are moral and ethical role models for us to follow, as Riess posits in *What Would Buffy Do?* In "The Freshman" (4.1), Xander proves that Buffy is a role model even within the canon of the show: "Buffy, I've gone through some fairly dark times in my life, faced some scary things, … when it's dark and I'm all alone and I'm scared or freaked out or whatever, I always think, 'What would Buffy do?' You're my hero." In his article, "Should We Do What Buffy Would Do?" Jason Kawal takes a different view from Xander and Riess, however. Kawal not only looks at the comparison of Buffy with Christ by parodying the pop culture riff, "what would Jesus do?" but also whether or not we should even be comparing ourselves to these figures.[10] Kawal establishes Buffy's status as a moral guide by looking at her in terms of heroic versus saintly actions, as defined by J.O. Urmson in "Saints and Heroes" (1958).[11] Heroic actions

---

9 Luke 6:37: Judge not, and ye shall not be judged: condemn not, and ye shall not be condemned: forgive, and ye shall be forgiven.

[10] Kawal's article appeared in Buffy the Vampire Slayer *and Philosophy: Fear and Trembling in Sunnydale* in 2003 and Riess' book was published in 2004. Though Riess is aware of the anthology and mentions various articles from it, she does not address Kawal or mention him, so it would not appear that his article had any direct influence on the construction of her work or argument.

[11] Urmson, J. O. "Saints and Heroes." *Essays in Moral Philosophy.* Ed. A.I. Melden. Seattle: U of Washington P, 1958. 198-216.

require a person to overcome significant fear[12] in order to perform a morally praiseworthy act, while saintly actions require a significant sacrifice or break from natural behaviors in order to perform a morally praiseworthy act (Kawal 150-151).

There is no doubt that Buffy performs both heroic and saintly actions; what Kawal takes issue with is the idea of comparing ourselves to Buffy as our moral and ethical role model because we (the regular, human audience) cannot measure up to Buffy. She is human, but she is also the Slayer. What she would do in any given situation does not necessarily apply to what we would do because we have different expectations, desires, drives and capabilities than she does. For example, if we were to ask "what would Buffy do?" when we came across a vampire (or perhaps even a random mugger), Buffy would use her Slayer abilities to take care of the situation and bring down the bad guy. But we do not have those abilities, so intervention by us would likely lead to injury or possibly death. Therein lies the issue of having Buffy as a moral guide.

Buffy exists on a different plane of morality than us, according to Kawal. It is not just that her actions are morally good, but what we deem as a morally righteous action falls into the realm of her duty as a Slayer, so it is not necessarily supererogatory – actions which are morally good and praiseworthy, but not morally required. This higher standard that she is held to is part of what elevates her to the status of a savior figure. As the Slayer, she is required by the nature of her position to fight the forces of evil and possibly die in that fight. But even more than that, she takes it upon herself to make sacrifices so others do not have to. In the Season 5 finale, "The Gift" (5.22) for example, Buffy throws herself into a (supposed) Hell dimension to save the world even when she does not have to. The portal could have

---

[12] This may also be adapted so that an action is considered heroic if it takes place in a situation where a normal person might feel fear (Kawal 150).

been closed with Dawn's blood as well as Buffy's. Dawn tries to sacrifice herself – following

Buffy's moral lead and knowing that it must be done in order for the world to survive – but

Buffy takes her place. She performs above and beyond even her own high standards of

morality in an act of salvation and sacrifice for her sister and her friends.

In the same episode, Buffy makes the morally superior decision not to kill the villain.

She has been battling the god Glorificus (aka Glory), viciously swinging a troll hammer at

her face, when Glory transforms into her human counterpart, Ben. Buffy immediately stops

her attack because she cannot harm a human.[13] Buffy lets Ben/Glory live and continues her

fight to save Dawn, prompting the following exchange between Giles and Ben:

> BEN: She [Buffy] could've killed me.
> GILES: No, she couldn't. And sooner or later Glory will re-emerge and make
> Buffy pay for that mercy – and the world with her. Buffy even knows
> that and still she couldn't take a human life. She's a hero, you see.
> She's not like us.

Buffy is held to a higher moral standard because of her Slayer status. This superiority

sometimes causes problems, both for those around her and for herself. She is not allowed to

make mistakes in judgment because they could literally mean the end of the world. In

"Surprise" (2.13) and "Innocence" (2.14), Buffy sleeps with her vampire lover, Angel,

unknowingly breaking the curse that granted him a soul and releasing the demonic Angelus,

who promptly tries to end the world. Buffy stops him, but she feels responsible for

unleashing Angelus, endangering others, and losing her lover – even though she had no idea

her actions would have such consequences. At the end of the episode, she sits with her

---

[13] It is actually part of the Buffyverse canon that Slayers are forbidden from killing humans, as discussed in "Gingerbread" (3.11) when Buffy asks Giles to find a loophole in the "Slayers don't kill people" rule so she can go after a supposed coven of witches who killed two children. Later, in "Bad Girls" (3.14) and "Consequences" (3.15), we see the mental and emotional toll that killing a human has upon a Slayer when Faith accidentally kills one of the Mayor's henchmen. It does not matter that the man killed is a villain – he was human, and therefore not part of the Slayer's duty.

Watcher, Giles, and says, "You must be so disappointed in me." She holds herself accountable. Giles, on the other hand, does not condemn her. Instead, he offers acceptance and, to some extent, forgiveness. He does not say that he forgives her in those exact words, but that he finds no guilt in her.

Forgiveness and redemption are found throughout *Buffy*, sometimes asked for, sometimes not. In "I Only Have Eyes for You" (2.19), Buffy is still reeling from finding out that she is responsible for the return of the sadistic Angelus and has a hard time forgiving herself mainly because she does not feel she deserves to be forgiven. Giles' description of forgiveness in this episode is one of the closest parallels of the Buffyverse and Christian principles when he says, "To forgive is an act of compassion, Buffy. It's not done because people deserve it. It's done because they need it." When Buffy questions why another character would forgive someone who hurt her, Giles asks the quintessential question, "Does it matter?" The answer is that the forgiveness was done out of love, a reflection of "For God so loved the world."[14]

This theme of forgiveness or mercy being given to those who may or may not deserve it is repeated in Season 7 in "The Killer in Me" (7.13) when a vengeance hex is placed on Willow and she slowly begins to turn into Warren, the man who killed Tara and whom Willow eviscerated. Amy, the girl who hexed Willow, is angry because Willow is still powerful and still welcomed by her friends even after the events of Season 6:

> AMY: Willow always had all the power … The rest of us, we had to work twice as hard to be half as good. But no one cares about how hard you work. They just care about cute, sweet Willow. … She gave in to evil – stuff worse than I can even imagine – She almost destroyed the world! And yet everyone keeps on loving her?

---

[14] John 3:16 – For God so loved the world that he sent his only begotten Son, that whosoever believeth in Him shall not perish, but have everlasting life.

Amy does not understand why or how Willow is forgiven. She is jealous of Willow's power, seeing it only as power to achieve, not the power she, herself, has to forgive. Amy was with Willow from the first time Willow began to experiment with magic in high school, and when Willow became addicted and turned to dark magic. She feels that she has not been forgiven – she does not benefit from the same sort of inclusion and support system that Willow does – so she hexes Willow to punish her.

Part of Amy's spell is that it allows the victim's subconscious to pick the form of the punishment so that it is more painful and personal. In this, we see that Willow has not completely forgiven herself for killing Warren and she does not feel she has earned the right to move on with her life. When she kisses Kennedy, one of the Potential Slayers, she admits that it causes her to forget about Tara – her lover killed by Warren – "just for a second … I let her be dead. She's really dead. And I killed her." The seventh season sees Willow constantly dealing with her guilt and need for forgiveness. We see Willow struggling with her magic and distrusting herself throughout the entirety of Season 7, up until she works a spell to unlock the Slayer power in all the Potential Slayers in "Chosen" (7.22). At that moment, she is bathed in white light and her hair turns white. This is a complete reversal from Dark Willow when her hair, eyes, and veins turn black. Kennedy, who is watching her perform the spell, says, "You are a goddess." Willow has been forgiven not only by those around her, but by herself, and she is made white and pure.[15]

---

[15] White is a symbol of purity in many legends, myths and faiths. For the Christian religion, specifically, the idea of being made pure and washed "white as snow" can be seen in Isaiah 1:18 – "Though your sins are like scarlet, they shall be as white as snow" – and Psalm 51:7 – "Purify me from my sins, and I will be clean; wash me, and I will be whiter than snow."

Willow is not the only one dealing with a need for forgiveness and redemption in the final season of *Buffy*. This last season begins with Buffy talking to Dawn, and The First talking to Spike, both expressing the idea that everything in life boils down to one truth – "it's about power" ("Lessons" 7.1). Buffy and The First have varying views of what that power should be, which I will examine in depth shortly, but one of the most frequent uses of power in Season 7 is the power of redemption and forgiveness (Riess 175).

In "Beneath You" (7.2) Spike, who had his soul returned to him at the end of Season 6, is dealing with the guilt and conscience of what he has done as a vampire for almost a century, including his attempted rape of Buffy. In a darkened church, he explains his pain to Buffy and walks towards a large white cross on the altar, saying "She shall look on him with forgiveness, and everybody will forgive and love. He will be loved." He sounds almost as if he is quoting scripture, petitioning for forgiveness, but it is clear he is speaking to and about Buffy. Spike embraces the cross, one arm on each cross bar, so that his body is draped across it and becomes the crucifix. As his body begins to smoke and sizzle, he asks, "Can we rest now? Buffy, can we rest?" Spike looks to Buffy for forgiveness – she is the reason he wanted his soul back in the first place, so he could be worthy of her – and speaks of her as a figure of salvation. His final question, asking for rest, sets Buffy up as capable of giving him respite. This is reminiscent of Jesus' words in Matthew 11:28: "Come to me, all you who are weary and burdened, and I will give you rest."

Later in the season, Buffy functions as a figure of salvation for Spike once again. In "Sleeper" (7.8), we learn that The First has been manipulating Spike to make him kill and sire vampires. The First lures both Spike and Buffy to where Spike has buried the bodies of his recent kills and tricks him into attacking her. However, when Spike tastes Buffy's blood, he awakens from The First's trance and stops fighting. None of the other times when Spike

has killed has the taste of human blood brought him out of his trance. There is something

particular about Buffy's blood that cleanses and saves him from himself.

This is not the first time that Buffy's blood is used for salvation (Wilson 148). There

is a running theme of Buffy's blood being the way out, the saving factor, which is one reason

why Riess identifies Buffy as a traditional Christ figure. In "Prophecy Girl" (1.12), Buffy's

blood is what allows The Master to be resurrected, and in "Graduation Day, Part 2" (3.22),

Buffy's blood saves Angel when he's been poisoned by Faith (the phrase carries quite the

symbolism). Buffy fully embodies the concept of salvation by blood in "The Gift" (5.22)

when she sacrifices herself to close the portal opened by Dawn's blood. It is established a

few episodes earlier, in the aptly titled episode "Blood Ties" (5.13), that Dawn shares

Buffy's blood. Dawn is made from Buffy, so Buffy can take her place and die to close the

portal. This is parallel to the Christian concept of Christ being human and humanity being

made in God's image.[16] This revelation of blood and its freeing power holds true for most of

the series, even when Buffy's blood is not involved. The Master is raised from a pool of

blood in the Hellmouth; Angel's blood both opens and closes the portal of the demon

Acathla; Faith's blood on her knife prompts the Mayor to chase Buffy to where a trap has

been laid for him. As Spike says, "it's always got to be blood … Blood is life" ("The Gift").

The Hellmouth, in particular, relies upon blood to be opened and activated. It is

opened at the start of Season 7 when Andrew kills Jonathan – both members of the Evil Trio

with Warren from Season 6 – and spills his blood upon the seal that covers the Hellmouth

---

[16] Genesis 1:27 – "So God created man in His own image; in the image of God, He created him; male and
female, He created them." Galatians 4:4-5 – "God sent forth His Son, born of a woman, born under the law, to
redeem those who were under the law, that we might receive the adoption as sons."

("Conversations with Dead People" 7.7). When it comes time to close the seal, however, it is not simply blood that is required. Buffy takes Andrew to the seal under the pretense that he will read an ancient magical text to close it, but when they get to the seal she says, "Doesn't make sense, does it? Bringing you here to talk to it [the seal]. This thing doesn't understand words, it understands blood." She tells him that the blood of the person who awoke it will close it, meaning that Andrew's blood must be spilled to close the seal. In a move that is more reminiscent of the Old Testament "Sinners in the Hands of an Angry God" religion than the all-merciful and forgiving New Testament Christ figure, Buffy literally holds Andrew over the glowing pit of hell with a knife to his throat:

> BUFFY: When your blood pours out, it might save the world. What do you think about that? Does it buy it all back? Are you redeemed?
> ANDREW: (*crying*) No.
> BUFFY: Why not?
> ANDREW: Because I killed him. … I killed Jonathan. And now you're gonna kill me. And I'm scared, and I'm going to die. And this – this is what Jonathan felt.[17]

When Andrew's tears fall upon the seal, it ceases to glow and hum. It has been closed. When Andrew expresses surprise, Buffy pulls the knife away and says that the seal "didn't want blood. It wanted tears." In this case, blood is not required – an acknowledgement of fault is. Andrew cries for what he has done, cries for forgiveness. While his tears close the seal, Andrew's forgiveness is not complete until the final episode of the series when Anya pushes him out of the way and sacrifices herself for him in the final battle. With her sacrifice – offering up her blood – he is deemed worthy and is saved.

Forgiveness and mercy in *Buffy* are sometimes easily given, but not easily earned or kept. They are fleeting, with each capable of being lost or retracted depending upon a

---

[17] Unlike the redemption by blood seen for other characters in the show, the blood sacrifice would not redeem Andrew here because it would be Buffy taking his life, not Andrew offering it up willingly.

character's actions. Unlike the traditional, unconditionl forgiveness of Christian belief, forgiveness in *Buffy* requires sacrifice and devotion – a promise to do better, blood, effort – and even then, it may not be complete. Spike, for example, fights numerous demonic trials in order to have his soul restored so that he can be forgiven, but he has to constantly work to achieve forgiveness. Dawn and Xander never fully trust him, and Giles and Wood even try to kill him for his past crimes rather than forgive him. It is not until he ultimately sacrifices himself in order to stop The First that he is redeemed. Like Willow, forgiveness is given to him from various sources, but it is only when he takes it upon himself that full forgiveness is achieved. Looking within for forgiveness instead of finding it in a religious savior or institution can be seen as a reflection of the religious uncertainty in society that is prompting the move to non-denominational churches. There is also the fear, deep down – even among believers – that the forgiveness of Christ is not truly enough. That it cannot cover all the sins we have committed. Seeing forgiveness as something that can be earned as opposed to freely given, allows us to see it as being attainable.

"The stake is not the power…"[18]

Access to forgiveness and salvation are two of the main foundations of power for the Christian Church. Battles over how salvation can be achieved have erupted within the Church and spilled out to ensnare the secular world as the Church fought to be the sole arbiter of forgiveness and salvation, thereby amassing a great deal of power within its relics, clergy and dogma. This power is almost exclusively patriarchal in nature – united under one male godhead, the Father, and accessible only through the male savior, the Son. Even before the addition of Christ to the faith, God could not be approached by regular, un-ordained people.

---

[18] "Lessons" (7.1)

Followers and believers had to go through priests and intermediaries who were allowed to go into the holy temples. As such, access to the Church has always relied upon the existing power structure of the patriarchal society.

This system of patriarchal power is the source of ongoing conflict in *Buffy*, established in the very first episode when the voice-over claims that the "chosen one" will stand "alone" against the forces of darkness. Before the episode is even half over, Buffy has aligned herself with Giles, Xander and Willow, as well as been introduced to Angel who helps her and calls himself a "friend." Buffy is not alone – she is not a single, solitary power. Instead, she is a leading figure of a group that shares responsibilities. She is conflict with the traditional power. In his article "It's All About Power," Kevin Durand identifies these competing forces in the Buffyverse as patriarchal power and shared power. For Durand, the patriarchal power is a power to overcome obstacles, coerce followers or destroy those who stand in the way by amassing power under one entity or being. Shared power, on the other hand, is the empowerment of all; it enables others to fully realize their potential (45). Those who employ and search for patriarchal power are usually associated with masculinity and brute force; they see those who share power as being weaker, inferior and feminine in nature.

Specifically, I argue that patriarchal power structures in *Buffy* can be viewed as a metaphor or symbol of the traditional, patriarchal power of the Church, specifically Christianity. The idea of one God – all powerful, almighty, and all-knowing – and a one and only savior in the form of Jesus Christ – *the* way, *the* truth, and *the* light – easily fits into Durand's definition of patriarchal power. In my discussion of Buffy as a Common Christ figure, one who is separate from the traditional idea of the Church and savior, she becomes the symbol of shared power. This becomes more evident as we see each Big Bad overcome not merely by a "David and Goliath battle to the finish," but through a joint effort of Buffy and her friends (Durand, "The Battle Against the Patriarchal Forces" 182).

Patriarchal power has several representations within *Buffy,* and not all of them are in the villain camp, though almost all the Big Bads of the series can be said to represent it. The Master, Angelus, the evil Mayor Richard Wilkins III, and Adam – the main villains for Seasons 1-4 – all represent the straightforward, oppressive, and sometimes misogynistic power of the patriarchy in both their actions and their titles. The Master is dominating, Angelus is "the sire" or father of Drusilla and Spike, the Mayor is demonically and politically powerful, and Adam refers us back to the very first man himself. Within these four characters we also have strong references to religious themes. In the New Testament, Jesus is referred to as "The Master" or "Master" by his followers on several occasions. Angelus not only still carries the anglicized version of his name – Angel – but one of his most heinous acts is committed within a confessional booth where he pretends to be a priest. And Adam not only carries the name of the first man on earth, but he fulfills the role of God in attempting to create living beings in his own image. These four examples do not mean that only men can be members of the patriarchal power, though that is the traditional association of the Church. The patriarchy is male/masculine in nature, but can be enforced by anyone attempting to consolidate power under one rule, even women.

In Season 5, for example, we have Glorificus (aka Glory), a god from an unknown hell dimension. She is extremely feminine in her desire for designer clothes and beauty products, but her method of ruling is decidedly patriarchal. She also has a masculine double in Ben, the male identity who shares her body. Ben, though powerless in terms of Glory's godlike abilities, exerts his own power over other characters, such as when he recaptures

Dawn in "The Gift" (5.22) instead of letting her go. In Season 6, we have a multitude of villains. The Trio – Warren, Andrew and Jonathan – are more annoying than evil when all together. When Warren separates himself, however, he reveals a truly misogynistic and controlling attitude towards women, to the point where he attempts to kill Buffy and accidentally kills Willow's girlfriend Tara instead.

This action sets up the third, major villain in the form of Dark Willow. Grief-stricken, Willow hunts down Warren and skins him alive, using her magic for revenge. Willow, who has been a part of Buffy's shared-power forces to this point, separates herself and seeks to take power alone in order to destroy the world to end her pain. The final season's main villain is technically gender neutral – The First. The First is the first evil, and though it has the power to appear as any person who has died, it usually appears as women – Buffy, Drusilla, Jenny Calendar, and a young Slayer Potential named Eve.[19] Even though The First has brief moments where it shares power with its main henchman, Caleb, the power is not distributed in the same way as Durand argues. For The First, Caleb is a tool – he can interact with the physical world and it cannot. So instead of sharing power with Caleb in the sense of enabling him and realizing his potential, The First is establishing him as a focus of its own patriarchal power.

As a servant of The First, Caleb is one of the least subtle characters in all the Buffyverse. Where other villains and examples of the patriarchy merely hint at Church power structures, Caleb blatantly drives these concepts into us like a knife sliding into our bellies – which is exactly how he is introduced to the series in "Dirty Girls" (7.18). Durand calls Caleb

---

[19] The First only appears as men 3 times. In the first episode, "Lessons" (7.1), The First appears as all the major male villains, save Angelus, in a speech – meaning that each male character appears for a few seconds – before finishing as Buffy. Then, throughout the season, it occasionally appears as Jonathan before appearing once in the guise of the misogynistic Caleb at the end of the season.

"too obvious," saying that he is "almost a caricature of the woman-hating, deeply patriarchal cleric" ("The Battle Against the Patriarchal Forces" 176). He has a point. Everything about Caleb is obvious, from his name – biblically, Caleb was one of the spies sent by Moses into Canaan, and so Caleb functions as The First's envoy in the physical world – to his deep, southern drawl, to his use of Christian fundamentalist dogma. When we first meet Caleb, he has picked up a Potential Slayer on the road and soon after begins to torture her by branding her neck with his heated ring. As the girl screams, he shouts, "That's it! That's a cleansing fire. Hallelujah!" But as much as he is a caricature, he is also a true representation of what society sees in the Church. He does not represent every church figure, but he does embody the most infamous, the ones that get noticed for all their misdeeds. When we see Caleb, we are not meant to see a mockery of the church, but the Church itself (Durand, "The Battle Against the Patriarchal Forces" 177). His constant degrading of Buffy – of women in general – along with his riffs on power and authority, make it clearer than almost any other force in *Buffy* that the patriarchy of the Church is something to be fought against.

All of the main villains throughout *Buffy* are examples of patriarchal power, which is partly why they always fail in their endeavors: their antiquated power structures are incapable of adapting to the shared power of Buffy and the Scoobies. But the villains are not the only examples of patriarchal power gone awry. There are also several groups and individuals who initially fall into the "good guy" camp that represent the patriarchy. They are not inherently evil all the time in the same way The Master, Adam or The First are, but it is important to note that when they do cross the line and become forces to be stopped or dealt with, they are at the height of their patriarchal power. The inclusion of such groups is important to note in our consideration of the idea of patriarchal power as being representative of the Church because it shows that *Buffy* is not trying to portray religion in a bad light. Instead, it is highlighting what can go wrong when people get caught up in the concept of tradition and rules to the point where they cannot see any other solution.[20] When Buffy and her group come in with a joint solution, they are not attempting to topple the patriarchal power of these groups. They often try to work with the organization in question, willing to share power with them as well to solve the problem.

The largest group that exists from the beginning until the end of the series is The Watchers' Council. This group would seem to be a key part of the shared power structure because their whole purpose is to watch, observe, record history, and train Slayers. It is a large group of people spread all over the world. We learn later in the series that the Watchers began as the Shadow Men, who created the First Slayer. Our main view into the Watchers is through Rupert Giles, Buffy's Watcher. Even though Giles eventually becomes a part of Buffy's collective forces, he starts off as an example of the traditional patriarchal structure in that he resists the inclusion of Xander and Willow in Buffy's world. He attempts to train Buffy in the traditional ways and, as she asserts her identity outside her role as the Slayer, he slowly begins to be more and more aligned with her idea of communal force.

The Watchers' Council, as a whole, however, becomes more and more patriarchal as the series progresses, both visually and thematically. Aside from a few brief scenes and the mention of a few female watchers who are violently killed off screen or turn out to be evil, the Council is almost entirely represented by men.[21] When they attempt to rein Buffy in

---

[20] I am not saying that *Buffy* was specifically created as a religious commentary, either pro or con. Joss Whedon, the creator of *Buffy*, is a professed atheist and has often commented that he actively tried to avoid religious themes. However, the power structures that are dealt with in the show are easily applied to a religious structure, even if he didn't intend them to be.

[21] Rhonda Wilcox's "Who Died and Made Her the Boss? Patterns of Mortality in *Buffy*" also looks at the representation of men in the Watchers' Council when she discusses patriarchal succession versus communal action.

under their direct power, she breaks away from them, recognizing that their patriarchal configuration does not serve the same views as she does. When the Council comes back in Season 5, they are more interested in reasserting their dominance over Buffy and her group than in stopping Glory. Their isolationistic power sense also results in their demise as they cut themselves off from all other helpful sources of power instead of sharing information.

This pattern of isolating themselves to the point of obsolescence or death in an attempt to exert a patriarchal power scheme also happens to several other groups. The school boards and administration try to enforce a patriarchal power structure upon the teachers, students and parents. As a result, Principals Flutie and Snyder are both eaten alive by aggressive forms of masculinity – a pack of hyena-spirit-infused teenagers, and a demonic politician who has just transmogrified into a giant snake. Parents and Parent Groups, such as Moms Opposed to the Occult (MOO) are perhaps the oldest and most recognized form of patriarchy in their attempts to enforce parental controls. The last two power centers that, at first, seem to be positive forces are Season 4's Initiative, a paramilitary group attempting to corral and control all the supernatural and demonic forces of the world, and the Shadow Men, the trio of men who originally created the first Slayer.

The Initiative is brought down by Adam, the demon-human-machine[22] hybrid, in his attempt to create a world full of creatures like him, because they refuse to share information and power with Buffy. In "Primeval" (4.21), Buffy and the Scoobies confront the general in charge of the Initiative's underground facility:

> COLONEL: You telling me my business?
> BUFFY: This is not your business. It's mine. You, the Initiative, the boys at
> the Pentagon – you're all in way over your heads. Messing with
> primeval forces you have absolutely no comprehension of.

---

[22] I say machine instead of cyborg because the elements Adam has are machine in nature as opposed to being human elements mechanized for use.

COLONEL: And you do?
BUFFY: I'm the Slayer. You're playing on my turf.
COLONEL: Up there, maybe. But down here, I'm the one who's in control.

Though Buffy uses possessive phrases ("not your business. It's mine. … You're playing on my turf," for example), she has come with the idea of shared power in mind. She has brought her friends to help her defeat Adam and is willing to work with the Initiative's soldiers if they will work with her. Even after it becomes clear that Buffy was right about Adam setting the Initiative up for slaughter, however, the colonel refuses to give up his identity of power and control which ultimately leads to his own death at the hands of an escaping demon. Buffy, through a spell that shares the powers and abilities of the Slayer and her core group of friends, defeats Adam and manages to save several soldiers.

In the final moments of the episode, a nameless officer sitting at a briefing table gives a voice-over description of the battle as scenes play out, including the death of the Colonel. He says that it is "only through the actions of the deserter [Riley] and a group of civilian insurrectionists" that they did not lose all of their forces. "I trust the irony of that is not lost on any of us," he continues, highlighting the point that if they had not attempted ultimate patriarchal control and had instead accepted Buffy on her own terms and the assistance she offered, there would not have been such a loss of life.

Through the Initiative, *Buffy* comments on the dangers of a government power that works "for the good of humanity" without having anyone to keep that power in check. When we also consider the Initiative as a metaphor of the patriarchal power of the Church, we get a similar warning against allowing any one religious power to rule unchecked. Almost every time religions split off into separate groups or sects, it is through the actions of a small group of people who are often branded as insurrectionists or heretics by the Church proper. If the

Church does not change, does not loosen its patriarchal hold and reliance on what many

modern parishioners view as outdated traditions, it is possible that their power will be

stripped as groups begin to break off. While we see later in the series that the Initiative is not

completely finished, their power has been greatly diminished in their role as a powerful

entity in the fight against demons. The very last line of dialog we get in the episode is from

the nameless officer as he pronounces the end of the Initiative: "The Initiative itself will be

filled in with concrete. Burn it down, gentlemen. Burn it down, and salt the Earth" and after

this pronouncement the screen goes black. Salting the Earth is a sign of cursing the land, the

idea being that once it is salted, nothing will grow from it.[23] Not only has the Initiative lost its

power, it can never fully regain it.

Out of all the representations of patriarchal power, however, the Shadow Men of "Get

It Done" (7.15) are possibly the most disturbing, even compared to the villains. The villains

at least establish themselves as evil, so we expect their behavior. The Shadow Men are set up

as a possible ally or source of knowledge for the Slayer as she prepares for her most difficult

battle yet. They are set up in the start of the episode as a possible mystical *deus ex machina*,

something that will give Buffy the edge she needs to win. She is given an "emergency kit"

that used to be passed down from Slayer to Slayer and is related to a Slayer's "power." Buffy

travels to meet the Shadow Men through a magical portal because what they have for her

cannot just be shown; the incantation says that she must "see," but only if she's "willing to

make the exchange." What that exchange is seems to be clear – Buffy goes to another

dimension and a demon comes to hers. When she comes back, the demon must be returned.

---

[23] The most famous instance of a conqueror salting the earth is when Carthage was sacked and then salted in the
Third Punic War, but there are also other instances, including a reference in Judges 9:45 when Abimelek salted
his own city after putting down a revolt.

But there is another meaning to that phrase: she must be willing to exchange part of herself for more power.

When Buffy goes to the Shadow Men to learn what she needs to know to fight, they tell her, "We cannot give you knowledge. Only Power." This is a huge red flag in terms of patriarchal versus shared power structures, especially when compared to another group we meet later in "End of Days" (7.21) – the Guardians. This is a group of women who worked in secret to forge a weapon for the Slayer line, specifically keeping their work hidden from the Shadow Men because they wanted the power to be given to those who need it instead of collected under those who would become the Watchers:

> BUFFY: [speaking of the Shadow Men] Yeah. Met those guys. Didn't really
> care too much for 'em."
> GUARDIAN: Ahh, yes. Then you know. And they became the watchers. And
> the watchers watched the Slayers. But we were watching them.
> BUFFY: Oh! So you're like… what are you?
> GUARDIAN: Guardians. Women who want to help and protect you.

The Shadow Men are the first Watchers, which explains where the latter get their stance on traditional power. They want to control and manipulate the Slayer and any information related to her. Even after being effectively cut off by Buffy in "Checkpoint" (5.12), the Watchers continue to try and reassert themselves into the Slayer's world as a source of power and control. The head of the Council, Quentin Travers, communicates almost entirely in militaristic or power-based terminology, using phrases like "first volleys," "operatives" and "visuals and tacticals – highest alert." In "Never Leave Me," (7.9) after The First's minions have attacked a Council stronghold, he tells the others not to worry, that "we are still masters of our fate, still captains of our souls." He makes plans to mobilize the remaining Watchers to go to Buffy in Sunnydale, because he realizes that is where the final battle is to take place. However, he is still looking at the situation in terms of patriarchal power, in the terms of the

Shadow Men. Instead of contacting Buffy and trading information, he plans to move his forces, like a commander, into battle. He exclaims, "These are the times that define us. Proverbs 24:6. O, by wise council, you shall make your war," before, somewhat unexpectedly, the entire Council building explodes.

This reliance on force and patriarchy is a direct link to the ways of power the Shadow Men possess and act on, and it is in direct contrast to the Guardians. The Guardian Buffy meets explains that they can give her a weapon, a mystical scythe, but she already has weapons. What Buffy needs is knowledge and help. The Shadow Men do not offer help or protection for Buffy. They knock her out, chain her to a cave floor and explain how they made the first Slayer – by chaining her in the same spot and forcing the essence of a demon into her. They are prepared to do the same thing to Buffy in an effort to solidify her power. This is the secondary meaning of the original incantation that allowed Buffy to open a portal to meet the Shadow Men: "You cannot just watch, but you must see. See for yourself, but only if you're willing to make the exchange" ("Get It Done"). She must be willing to exchange part of her humanity for the power of the demon in order to become stronger. When Buffy questions their methods, they simply say "This is how it was then. How it must be now" ("Get It Done"). They are not open to the idea of evolution or a change but constantly compare Buffy to the First Slayer, saying "the First Slayer did not talk so much" ("Get It Done"). Everything for them is power, gathered under one central being – the Slayer they have created.

In the case of the Shadow Men, the idea of patriarchal power being directly linked to the idea of masculine power and masculine identity is not subtle, especially when it is later contrasted with the all-female Guardians. It is overt in everything they do, from creating the

Slayer through demon rape to refusing to allow Buffy to question them. They tell Buffy that she does not understand, but she responds, "No, you don't understand! You violated that girl" ("Get It Done"). Then, Buffy breaks free and defeats two of the three men before walking up to the main Shadow Man and breaking in half the long staff he holds. To hammer home the idea of a broken symbol of phallic power, Buffy quips, "I knew it. It's always the staff." The Shadow Men only offer the traditional patriarchal version of power and control – "We offered you power," he says before Buffy leaves. The Shadow Men view the fight between the Slayer and the demons as always a "force against force struggle, a dualistic conflict between equal powers, a battle that plays by all the rules of the patriarchy" (Durand "It's All About Power" 55). This dichotomy of power and conflict is an echo of Travers' speech about going to battle with The First.

The Shadow Men and the Watchers, together, are perhaps the patriarchal powers in *Buffy* in which it is easiest to see a reflection of the Church. The Shadow Men forced power into the First Slayer by having a demon rape her. The act almost parallels the idea of the Immaculate Conception from which the birth of the savior occurs. Out of the First Slayer comes the line of Slayers – the Chosen Ones.[24] The Watchers are the modern Church equivalent of the older, traditional Shadow Men. The Watchers seem incredibly harsh and unyielding in their beliefs and practices, but once we meet the Shadow Men, we realize just how much they have mellowed. They are still patriarchal in nature, but not to the extent of

---

[24] An interesting side discussion in terms of looking at the Shadow Men as a version of the early church is why they bestowed this power of salvation – the power to fight demons – upon a girl instead of a male warrior. Part of this could be that the ideas of life and creation are inherently feminine. Elisabeth Bronfen examines something similar in *Over Her Dead Body*, explaining that in various myths and legends, a woman is often sacrificed to return the world to order and banish chaos (27-35). The idea of a demon infusing a man with power in the terms the way of the First Slayer is decidedly sexual. There is no shortage of feminist readings of *Buffy*, and several look at the Shadow Men's somewhat misogynistic attitudes, but very few do so through a religious lens.

their ancestors. Our discovery of the Shadow Men is equal to the discovery of long, lost texts or biblical records that, when rediscovered, change our interpretation of the Church.

Amongst all these examples of patriarchal power have been hints and mentions of the shared power of Buffy and her friends as they work in reaction to the patriarchal tradition. If we see the patriarchal power as the traditional church, then Buffy's pattern of sharing power sets her apart from them. Instead of just being a Christ figure of the modern world, she functions in an entirely separate power dynamic – she is a new savior. She works outside of Church/authority and tries desperately to maintain her humanity, frequently insisting that she's "just a girl."

Buffy functions as a Common Christ partially because of this aspect of communal power and distance from patriarchal authority. She is *the* Slayer, much in the tradition of the one and only Christ savior-figure, but she is not alone in preparing for, and fighting, battles. This is what sets her apart from the traditional patriarchal forces, even including the First Slayer. When she was created, the First Slayer lost elements of her humanity and became a primal force. She was a direct line of the Shadow Men's power – single, alone, and patriarchal. Since then, the Slayers were supervised, trained and prepared by the Watchers so that they all embody that same patriarchal understanding of power and control, with few exceptions. Though they retain their humanity unlike the First Slayer, they are still representative of that power and tradition.

At the end of Season Four, after having participated in a spell that allows Buffy, Willow, Xander and Giles to join their essences together to become one fighting force of conjoined power, Buffy meets the essence of the First Slayer in a dream. The First Slayer appears specifically in response to Buffy sharing her power with the others, something which

Giles identifies as being an insult to the source of the Slayer's power. She tells Buffy that to be a Slayer is to be "absolute" and "alone" ("Restless" 4.22). Buffy explains that she is different, that the world has changed. The First Slayer replies, "The Slayer does not walk in this world," an echo of biblical teachings that Christ and believers are set apart from the world of the flesh. In John 17:16, as Christ prays for his disciples he says, "They are not of the world, even as I am not of it." Another reference is in 1 John 2:15 when John speaks to believers: "Do not love the world or the things in the world. If anyone loves the world, the love of the Father is not in him." Buffy battles back against these ideas in her response: "I walk. I talk. I shop, I sneeze."

Buffy lives in the world she fights to save. She is not separate from it in any way. She has distanced herself from the controlling power of the Watchers and the tradition of the Slayer line and found a new way. She tells the First Slayer, "There's trees in the desert since you moved out. And I don't sleep on a bed of bones," to which the First Slayer angrily replies, "We… Are… Alone." Times have changed. Much like the Watchers reveal how tradition and practice (i.e. the Church) has changed, Buffy is an example of that change from the First Slayer. She has friends and family – she is human. She is still the savior figure responsible for the salvation of the world, but she does not live by the same patriarchal codes as the First Slayer. Buffy eventually dispels the First Slayer by telling her that she is not the source of Buffy's power or identity. Buffy is separate from her.

The idea of collective power represented by Buffy is not limited simply to joining spells and essences. The presence of friends and family beside her in the battle, or researching information and tactics beforehand, is what has allowed Buffy to live as long as she has in a role that has a short life expectancy. Even when Buffy dies, part of the reason for her resurrections is that she has friends to help her. In "Prophecy Girl" (1.12), Buffy is bitten by the Master and left to drown in a pool of water. She is saved because Xander and Angel come to help her and Xander is able to perform CPR on her. When she dies again at the end of Season 5 in "The Gift" (5.22), she is resurrected through Willow's magic at the start of Season 6. In the long line of Slayers, there has never been one who died and was resurrected, mainly because the Slayer always fought alone. When vampires and demons discover that Buffy is not alone, they are surprised. In "School Hard" (2.3), Spike's debut episode, he attempts to kill Buffy at Parent-Teacher night, but is unable to manage it because Buffy's friends help her, culminating in Buffy's mother, Joyce, hitting Spike over the head with an axe. Later in the episode as he plans his next attack he says, "A Slayer with family and friends. That sure as hell wasn't in the brochure." Buffy survives and succeeds not solely because of her inherent Slayer powers, but because she has people who help share some of her responsibility.

In Season 6 the idea of shared power is so prevalent that Buffy does not actually save the world herself. Instead, Buffy, her younger sister Dawn, vengeance demon Anya, friend Xander, and mentor Giles all work together to prevent the end of the world. When Willow's girlfriend, Tara, is killed in "Seeing Red" (6.19), Willow goes into a grief-fueled rage and absorbs dark magic, becoming Dark Willow, the main villain for the final episodes of the season. It is quickly established that Buffy will not be able to defeat Dark Willow on her own, especially since Buffy does not want to kill Willow. Dark Willow is an equal match for Buffy's Slayer-enhanced strength. During a physical fight, Dark Willow tells Buffy, "I get it now. The Slayer thing really isn't about the violence. It's about the power" ("Two to Go" 6.21). It takes the combined efforts of Buffy and her friends to contain Dark Willow, with

Anya chanting a Sumerian protection and binding spell to keep Dark Willow from using her magic to harm anyone. When that fails, Giles shows up with magical powers he has borrowed from a powerful coven – as a direct counterpart to Dark Willow who has killed others or stolen her magical boosts – which work to bind Dark Willow for a brief period. Eventually, Dark Willow drains Giles of his powers, too, and goes off to destroy the world.

With Anya weakened, Buffy and Dawn trapped in a tomb fighting golems, and Giles unconscious, there is only Xander left to stop Dark Willow. He does not stop her through violence or magic – instead, he stops her with unconditional love (Riess 11). Xander tells her that no matter what she does, whether it is being his friend or destroying the world, he loves her and will always be there for her. Dark Willow scoffs at him, "Is this the master plan? You're going to stop me by telling me you love me?" ("Grave" 6.22). And yet it works. Dark Willow attempts to move Xander out of the way, tossing him about and lacerating his face and chest, but each time he comes back to stand before her. And each time, her magic becomes weaker and weaker as he repeats that he loves her until she finally collapses in tears at his feet. He kneels with her as the dark magic drains from her body.

In this moment, we have something of a traditional Christ figure in Xander. Xander has spent most of Season 6 working as a handyman. When he first appears before Dark Willow, she tells him to leave and he refuses, saying, "You're not the only one with powers, you know. You may be a hopped-up uber-witch, but this carpenter can dry-wall you into the next century" ("Grave"). Xander identifies himself as a powerful carpenter, mostly in jest, but the symbolism is not lost in the joke. In Xander, we have a peaceful figure, a carpenter, who saves the world through an act of unconditional and selfless love – a direct correlation to the salvation of Christ. Even though Xander is alone with Willow at the end, he is only able to be successful through the actions of others, specifically Giles. Part of Giles' plan was to exhaust her magic to the point where she would have to drain his power to recharge. He says that his powers were "the true essence of magic," where Dark Willow's magic "came from a place of rage and power" ("Grave"). Once again, we have a discussion of the negative aspects of this type of power. The forces she takes from Giles reawaken her humanity which is what allows Xander to reach her, the true Willow beneath all the rage and grief. So even when we have a more traditional Christ figure – as close to an actual Christian reference with Xander as a carpenter and the use of the Prayer of Saint Francis of Assisi over the montage of scenes of all the main characters – he is only successful because of everyone's collective effort.

The ultimate moment of unity comes in the final season when Buffy has Willow cast a spell that activates the Slayer power within all the potential Slayers around the world. As she explains what is going to happen, Buffy specifically identifies the battle against the patriarchal tradition that she is proposing:

> BUFFY: So here's the part where you make a choice. What if you could have that power, now? In every generation, one Slayer is born, because a bunch of men who died thousands of years ago made up that rule. They were powerful men. This woman [Willow] is more powerful than all of them combined. So I say we change the rule. I say my power, should be *our* power. Tomorrow, Willow will use the essence of this scythe to change our destiny. From now on, every girl in the world who might be a Slayer, will be a Slayer. Every girl who could have the power, will have the power. Can stand up, will stand up. Slayers, every one of us. Make your choice. Are you ready to be strong? ("Chosen" 7.22)

This is not simply a battle tactic to defeat The First. This is a decisive action to change the rules of power governing the Slayers. In so doing, she proposes an even larger split than she herself has achieved numerous times by "quitting" the Council ("Graduation Day, Parts I &

II 3.21-3.22), telling the Council not to interfere in her business ("Checkpoint" 5.12), and refusing to allow the Shadow Men to infuse her with demonic power ("Get It Done" 7.15). She is effectively abandoning all ties with the traditional, patriarchal heritage of the Slayer line.

The final season starts with Buffy telling Dawn that even though she has a stake, "the stake is not the power" ("Lessons" 7.1):

> BUFFY: Who's got the power, Dawn?
> DAWN: Well, I've got the stake.
> BUFFY: The stake is not the power. … Who's got the power?
> DAWN: He does.
> BUFFY: Never forget it. Doesn't matter how well prepped you are or how
> well armed you are. You're a little girl.
> DAWN: Woman.
> BUFFY: Little woman.
> DAWN: I'm taller than you.

Here we see a foreshadowing of the final strategy of the series, to empower all women. Buffy tells Dawn the stake is not the source of the power, a move that will be echoed when Buffy breaks the Shadow Man's staff in "Get It Done" and jokes about the phallic nature of the power staff. The stake, the phallic symbol of penetration, is not the power. And though Dawn is young, a little girl (woman), she quickly points out that she is physically bigger/taller than Buffy. The "little woman" – Buffy – has the power. And she is ready to share it.

During "Chosen," as Buffy's speech is given in full in a voice-over, we see scenes not only of the Potential Slayers but of women and girls all around the world receiving power. Some are playing sports, some are at family dinners, and at least one is being attacked by an abusive boyfriend. One by one, they breathe deep, taking in their new power, standing tall and strong. The abused girl, in particular, catches the arm of the man hitting her and holds him away. It is not simply the battle with The First that is affected by the distribution of the

Slayer's power to all Potentials – it is a global change in traditional power structures

(Atchley 89). In *Buffy*, power has never been limited solely to Buffy herself, nor to a single

line of inheritance (Wilcox, "Who Died and Made Her the Boss?" 5).[25] She establishes

herself early on as a new brand of Slayer, one who is not content with traditional models.

Though the prophecy of the Slayer states that there will be only one girl, one "Chosen" girl to

face the darkness, when Buffy dies, suddenly there are two Slayers in existence at the same

time. A radically new line of Slayers begins alongside Buffy that breaks with all the previous

patriarchal traditions of power (Durand, "The Battle Against the Patriarchal Forces" 180).

When she dies and prompts the calling of a second Slayer, that tradition is broken, but not

----

[25] There are a few cases where Buffy falls back into the traditional power structures, and in each of these instances, she loses something precious to her. The best examples of how *Buffy* shows that Buffy is not meant to be a power unto herself come at the end of Season 2 and beginning of Season 3. Buffy must battle her former lover Angel, now in the guise of the evil Angelus. She receives a visit from a demon named Whistler who tells her, "In the end you're always by yourself – you're all you've got" ("Becoming, Part II" 2.22). Throughout "Becoming, Parts I & II" (2.21-2.22) and the beginning of Season 3's "Anne" (3.1) and "Dead Man's Party" (3.2), Buffy works alone with varying degrees of success. She defeats Angelus only to have to sacrifice Angel as Willow works a spell from her hospital bed to restore his soul. Buffy runs away to Los Angeles and gets dragged into a hell dimension before fighting her way out with a group of other runaway teens who were taken as easy prey. When she finally returns to Sunnydale in "Dead Man's Party," she must deal with the fallout of going alone and attempt to repair the relationships with her mother and friends while fighting a horde of zombies. In each episode, Buffy is victorious in her ultimate battle, but she is not content. Her world is not made better for her victories. These four episodes show that going alone, working under one's own power instead of through shared power, may be heroic in nature, but in essence will result in being dragged to hell and having to fight back out again (Wilcox, "Who Died and Made Her the Boss?" 7).

Faith has been called Buffy's shadow self by several critics because she is basically a polar opposite of Buffy for a large portion of the series. This includes feeling her Slayer power as a right, as something that is solely hers. As such, we get to see in Faith what would happen should a Slayer completely embrace the patriarchal notion of power and become a power unto herself. Faith joins the evil Mayor Wilkins and becomes consumed by the idea of singular power to the point that she does not question him or her role. This is in direct contrast to Buffy, who we see constantly questioning the Council, the Initiative, the Shadow Men, etc. It gets so bad that Faith eventually reaches a point where she can kill a man and simply say "Boss wants you dead" and when he asks why, she answers "you know, I never thought to ask" (Graduation Day, Part I 3.21). Faith is a version of the "unquestioning service of the power structure … for the sake of the approval, comfort and support of the father" (Wilcox, "Who Died and Made Her Boss?" 14). And just as Buffy's journey through the four episodes ending and beginning Seasons 2 and 3, Faith's journey into the traditional power structures shows us that the communal power of *Buffy* is a stronger path; "working alone, Faith has failed," Wilcox argues, which also highlights an interesting connection to the commentary on religion given Faith's name. Faith/faith has not succeeded on its own. Faith has a long road back to redemption, involving a trip to Los Angeles to visit Angel and going to prison for her crimes. When she returns to *Buffy* in Season 7, it is not in a search for power but out of a desire to help, to be a part of the group.

gone. The new line of Slayers that begins with Kendra and Faith is still somewhat under the patriarchal control of the Council. But when Willow's spell grants the Slayer power to every woman, every Potential, the patriarchal power structure is completely severed.

In the final moments of the series, the characters are gathered around Buffy looking at the crater where Sunnydale used to be and discussing what they need to do next, such as locating all the newly created Slayers and explaining what has happened to them. Willow asks Buffy what she thinks they should do and Faith says, "Yeah, you're not the one and only chosen anymore. You just gotta live like a person. How's that feel?" ("Chosen" 7.22), before the camera shows a close-up of Buffy's face as she begins to smile and then fades to black.

Buffy starts out as a Christ figure, a distinct figure of power and salvation, then becomes a Common Christ, more human but still different from almost everyone around her. But now, there are hundreds, thousands of her. She's "just a girl," and no longer the sole one responsible for saving everyone. That Faith is the one to say this line is important in terms of our discussion of how *Buffy* shows us the separation of the Common Christ from the patriarchal authority of the Church. We have now been told by faith/Faith that we don't have a one and only "chosen" savior anymore; we are responsible for our own salvation.

Once Willow's spell hits, the entire structure of power is changed. Power is no longer "limited to a single line" from one Slayer to the next (Wilcox, "Who Died and Made Her the Boss?" 5). Where traditional Christian teachings say that Christ is "*the* way" to salvation, we now have thousands of figures of strength and sacrifice created as Slayers, as girls/women who "make a choice ... to be strong." Buffy will always be *the* Slayer for our canon, partly because she is the center of the show, but also because she is the start of this new line of power, but she is no longer the only one who can save the world. Her status as *the* Slayer is a bit honorary at the series' end. *Buffy* obliterates the patriarchal power of a singular line of

salvation, as represented by the smoking crater that used to be Sunnydale/the Hellmouth, and

leaves in its place something new: a shared power of redemption and salvation.

"Where do we go from here?"

> "Where do we go from here?
> The battle's done and we kind of won
> So we sound our vict'ry cheer.
> Where do we go from here?"[26]

In the opening episode of Season 4, a girl asks Buffy "Have you accepted Jesus Christ

as your personal savior?" Buffy stutters and replies, "You know, I meant to and then I just

got really busy" ("The Freshman" 4.1). She has been busy saving the world, being a figure of

salvation and sacrifice. While this is meant as a comic statement, it also stands out as one of

the few, direct references to specific religion that we get in *Buffy*. Making it even more

significant is that Buffy says this while "wearing a crucifix given to her by Angel – a crucifix

that has saved her life in the past" (Erikson 110). The cross she wears is not associated with

Christ or Christianity by Buffy or by almost anyone in the Buffyverse. It is basically an

empty symbol of tradition – both in terms of religion and the lore of vampires being repelled

by crosses. The power it receives is from Buffy herself, not Christ.

The emptiness of the cross as a religious symbol does not mean that we cannot see

Christian symbols elsewhere in *Buffy*. In his article, "Sometimes You Need a Story:

American Christianity, Vampires and *Buffy*," Gregory Erikson specifically asks whether a

demonic presence – which *Buffy* has in spades – requires "at least an implied Christian one?

Can we have an evil without a sacred?" (114).[27] In a larger context, this is where many

---

[26] "Once More with Feeling" (6.7)

[27] We will see this question of whether the presence of demons and dark forces automatically means that there is
a God more directly referenced in *Supernatural*, specifically through the character of Dean.

Americans find themselves today. We see the negative, dark spaces of the world, some of which are connected to the Church, the supposed houses of the Lord and find ourselves unsure of whether we should trust them with our salvation.

Buffy subtly addresses this concern, offering us a Common Christ figure who questions the traditional power and offers forgiveness and salvation we can earn and take care of ourselves. *Buffy* acknowledges that these ideas are somewhat nebulous and hard to grasp; the show exists in the grey areas of certainty that the Church expresses in black and white – "I am the way, the truth and the life. No one comes to the Father except through me." Instead, Buffy offers us to share in her power without directly confronting or calling religious beliefs into play. Erikson claims that the world of experience in *Buffy* is "always on the edge or in the gaps of perception" (118). In the next chapter, I look at how *Supernatural* embodies the Common Christ and directly confronts Christianity. There are no hints or gaps. Instead of merely seeing the supernatural elements of religion in *The X-Files,* and beginning to question the foundational elements of power and forgiveness in *Buffy*, *Supernatural* directly examines the role of religious sacrifice and salvation in small-town, *Everyman* America, as seen through the windshield of a 1965 black Chevy Impala.

Chapter Four: "'If I don't save everyone, then no one will, and we all die'":

Death, Sacrifice, and Christianity in *Supernatural*

Figure 3: Crucifixion – "Dean on the Impala" – *Supernatural* promotional photo[1]

The Road So Far…

Starting in 2005, *Supernatural* obviously had connections to the previous WB hit,

Buffy, the Vampire Slayer. Whether it wanted those connections or not, it was hard to dismiss

another show that featured "attractive young people killing monsters" without at least

thinking about *Buffy* (Borsellino 107). In fact, the whole entertainment industry was wrapped

up in the fervor that *Buffy* and *The X-Files* had created a few short years before. On almost

every channel there was some show that centered on "ghosts, monsters and demons being

battled by super-powered heroes with expensive tech or a huge arsenal" (Chambers 165). On

Supernatural, the heroes were not necessarily super-powered, though there were moments

---

[1] "Dean on the Impala" – *Supernatural* promotional photo [Photography]. 24 October 2013.

that they received an other-worldly boost. Instead, *Supernatural* boasted two brothers, Sam and Dean Winchester, who drove around the country in an old muscle car (a 1967 Chevy Impala, to be exact) destroying ghosts, monsters and demons with whatever they had at hand. Sometimes they were aided by the people they were trying to save, or by fellow hunters, and eventually by Castiel, a bonafide angel of the Lord. But for the majority of the show's continuing run, it has just been Sam and Dean in the Impala with a map, some news-clippings about strange murders and all the best of mullet rock playing from the tape deck because, as Dean so eloquently puts it, in his car, "the driver picks the music. Shotgun shuts his cakehole" ("Pilot" 1.1).[2]

Monster-killing premise aside, *Supernatural* shared quite a large connection to both *Buffy* and *The X-Files*, ranging from borrowed storylines ("What Is and What Should Never Be" 2.20 was inspired by the *Buffy* episode, "Normal Again" 6.17) to shared writers and crew members (Knight, *The Official Guide: Season 2* 104). The writers of *Supernatural* would frequently give a tip of the hat to *The X-Files* through script references, including having Dean call a pair of federal agents he sees Mulder and Scully in the "Pilot" and later having him tell a bystander, "*The X-Files* is a TV show. This is real" ("Monster Movie" 4.5). *Supernatural* had a bit more in common with the earlier *The X-Files* in that it tended to go darker than *Buffy* did. Even the show's initial narrative arc of finding the demon who killed Sam and Dean's mother was reminiscent of Mulder's search for information about what happened to his sister (Abbott xi).

Supernatural is currently filming its ninth season and is contracted for a tenth. The original story about a yellow-eyed demon who pinned the Winchesters' mother to the ceiling

---

[2] All dialogue is taken from episode transcripts compiled by *Supernatural Wiki.*

and burned her has long been sorted out and a new mythology is being explored on the show

that is extremely heavy in Christian mythology and angel lore. For the purposes of this

dissertation, I am limiting my examination of *Supernatural* to the first five seasons. This is

partially because trying to analyze an on-going (and therefore ever changing) text is

incredibly difficult and lends itself to problems. The main reason, however, is because the

show was originally conceived to tell a five-season story arc by creator Eric Kripke (Abbott

xiv). Seasons 6 and beyond are a new story arc, one that continues and connects to the first

five years, but does not have the same approach or focus.

It is also within the first five seasons of *Supernatural* that we get to see Sam and

Dean explore the foundations of religion and go through the discovery that God is real and so

are angels, along with Lucifer. As I have previously stated, I wish to examine the presence

and treatment of religion and Christ figures in shows that are not inherently Christian by

nature. For the first three seasons, *Supernatural* has a relationship with Christianity similar to

Buffy in that it uses elements of Christian mythology without necessarily embracing

Christianity. Demons flinch at the name of Christ (Cristo), and holy water purifies weapons

and repels any number of evil beasts. There is a direct reference to the idea of hell and

torment, complete with demons, fire, torture and hellhounds. The direct concept of heaven,

salvation and Christ, however, are strictly listed as myth by the show's characters, the

demon-hunting brothers Dean and Sam Winchester.

Starting in the fourth season, however, and continuing on through the current ninth

season, the show has become specifically focused on Christian mythology. Sam and Dean

have both functioned as minor sacrificial figures in the first three seasons, suffering and

sacrificing to defeat evil and protect the people of the world. After dying at the end of the third season and going to hell, Dean is rescued and resurrected to his body by Castiel, an angel of the Lord, in order to stop the apocalypse and prevent the rising of Lucifer. From this point on, the show's canon includes demon and angel interaction, prophets of God (one of whom, Chuck, writes a series of books called *Supernatural* that Castiel calls "The Winchester Gospel"), the rising of Lucifer, the four horsemen of the apocalypse and other Revelation-based encounters. There is even one episode in which the deities and figures from other religions – such as Ganesh, Kali and Odin – gather to discuss the ongoing Judeo-Christian apocalypse.

When the apocalypse is thwarted at the end of Season 5 (spoilers), the original arc of the show ended. From that point on, *Supernatural* has explored a Heaven in turmoil from an absent God and a Hell up for new management with Lucifer locked away along with a whole slew of angels and demons who were all set for a major battle of apocalyptic proportions that never occurred. In short, the show that had no Christian ties at all when it began has become decidedly reliant upon Christian mythology for its storyline. This means that the impetus of the show has changed from Season 6 onward and it is not looking at Christianity the same way that it does in the first five seasons, which means that the latter seasons do not really fulfill what I am trying to accomplish. For these reasons, I have decided to only look at Seasons 1-5.

"Where's God in all this?"[3]

In 2009, a conservative Christian fundamentalist critic, S.T. Karnick, claimed that *Supernatural* displays a "clearly Christian" and "pro-Christian" message because Seasons 4 and 5 were focused on a biblical apocalypse and "spiritual war" (qtd in Giannini 163). It is

---

[3] "Lucifer Rising" 4.22

unclear whether or not Karnick actually watched any episodes or merely read summaries and reviews to know that this storyline was occurring, but there is hardly anything pro-Christian about the presence of God and angels on *Supernatural*. However, for a brief period of time it was one of the few popular shows on that displayed a constant reference to Christianity. Erin Giannini and Line Nybro Petersen argue that all the other religious folklore used alongside Christianity in *Supernatural*, combined with the negative portrayal of Christianity, show that *Supernatural* cannot be considered to be decidedly Christian (Giannini 164). I disagree, however, because even though it does negatively portray it and reference other religions, over the course of five seasons, Christianity is shown to be a dominant force. It is at least as equal in power, if not more powerful, than any other religion mentioned on the show. For example, in the episode "Hammer of the Gods" (5.19), several "pagan"/non-Christian gods gather to discuss the impending Judeo-Christian apocalypse. They plan to force Lucifer and Michael to, essentially, stop bickering and stop the apocalypse. However, when the angel Gabriel hears of this plan, he says that it will never work because Lucifer will simply turn all the other gods into "finger paint." There is no consideration that Lucifer will be weaker than all of the others combined. One of the most powerful gods present, Kali, calls Sam, Dean and Gabriel "arrogant" for their belief that Lucifer will be stronger, and yet it proves true. With barely a snap of his fingers, Lucifer destroys all the other religions present. This is not to say that more powerful means better, just that there is an obvious bias towards Christianity as being the most powerful religion.

As the total destruction of all other religions might insinuate, *Supernatural* does not hold a very high opinion of the organized realm of religion, especially Christianity. As Erica Engstrom and Joseph M. Valenzano claim, *Supernatural* "treats organized religion and individuals organized around religion as, at best, deluded, and at worst, hypocritical and evil"

(qtd in Simmons 164). Where *The X-Files* focuses on the supernatural elements of faith and

Christianity, *Buffy* subtly questions the ruling power structures of Christian authority and

forgiveness. *Supernatural*, however, is straightforward in its approach to Christianity. In the

Supernatural universe, the main figures of Christianity are a negative force. In much the

same way that Anderson says religion is often demonized in the Buffyverse, one of the

quickest ways to make audiences wary of a character on *Supernatural* is to have that

character be directly related to the Church. This is not true for all religious figures of course,

but even if we come across a religious figure who is not evil in some aspect, we can almost

be assured that they are surrounded by evil or at the very least that their beliefs run so firm

and strict that they refuse to accept any outside information. As Dean says about angels in

"It's the Great Pumpkin, Sam Winchester" (4.7), "They are 'righteous.' That's sort of the

whole problem. There's nothing more dangerous than some righteous a-hole who thinks he's

on a mission from God." Even though Sam and Dean's fight against demons and dark

supernatural forces often mimics the philosophical lines of Christianity, they are seen as

being separate from it.

There are many ways in which Christianity exists with *Supernatural* that are not overt

or negative. Almost all of the main characters carry some sort of biblical or religious name –

John, Samuel, Castiel; even Dean is religious, with "dean" being an older name for a deacon

or father of the church. There are also the obvious comparisons of Christ in the repeated

sacrifices, deaths and resurrections, from Sam and Dean specifically. When Dean is

resurrected by Castiel in "Lazarus Rising" (4.1), he has to convince Bobby that it truly is him, so he cuts himself with silver and allows Bobby to feel the wounds to see that they're

real, thereby re-enacting the scene of Doubting Thomas after Christ's return.[4]

In terms of the Common Christ theme, *Supernatural* rounds out the subtle attacks on

the church's patriarchal power that we see in *Buffy* by directly confronting Christianity and

then examines the uniqueness of the Christ figure by having the main characters die multiple

times as acts of sacrifice and get resurrected each time, thereby taking away some of the

specialness of the situation. With a character who can seemingly never stay dead, the idea of

everlasting life – the gift of Christ – becomes less of a gift and more of a burden. The

commonness of the action of sacrifice taken by Sam and Dean as Common Christs all but

demystifies the aura of death surrounding the sacrifice. Instead, we are left with two very

human heroes who, while willing to die and sacrifice themselves for the sake of humanity, do

so with no intention of being repaid and no affiliation with a church, religion or greater

power.

"So what do you say we kill some evil sons of bitches and we raise a little hell, huh?"[5]

In one of the quieter scenes of "Good God, Y'all," the second episode of

Supernatural's fifth season, a group of men and women sit in a dimly lit church basement

trying to figure out the truth behind an epidemic of demon activity in a small town. Dean

stands up and retrieves a bible from a shelf and begins to read from Revelation. After a few

moments of exposition, the preacher looks over at Dean and asks, voice incredulous, "Wait,

just back up. It's the apocalypse?" Dean looks at him, one eyebrow raised slightly, and

deadpans, "Sorry, Padre." The camera lingers on the preacher's face, showing his shock and

disbelief, before the scene ends. In the climax of the episode, the groups of townspeople are

---

[4] See John 20:24-29.
[5] "Magnificent Seven" (3.1)

fighting each other, each believing the other to be possessed by demons. During the fight, the

first and only casualty is the preacher, shot through the chest as he runs towards shelter. One

girl cries out for him and rushes to see if he's alive, but his death is quickly overshadowed as

another part of the fight takes over the scene. The preacher is never mentioned again as the

episode moves on to the brotherly drama of the main characters Dean and his brother Sam.

Exchanges like this, where the authority figures of religion or the church seem

astounded that the tenets of their religion – especially the unseemly aspects like demons, the

devil, possession or the apocalypse – actually exist, are common in many *Supernatural*

episodes, as well as several other facets of entertainment. Part of this surprise serves as comic

interjection. We enjoy seeing their confusion and uncertainty because the church is

advertised in Hollywood as being led by righteous and all-knowing individuals. Another

aspect derived from that confusion is that it sets up the (usually) non-religious/layperson in a

position of knowledge and power over the church. They know the demons/devils/etc. are

real, but when they go to the church, they are seen as mentally unstable. This sets up the

layperson as the misunderstood hero, the one not bound by religious law or doctrine,

therefore making him or her more likeable by American audiences. An example of this

scenario from film is *Hellraiser III: Hell on Earth* (1992) when Joanne "Joey" Summerskill

runs into a church and screams that "they're" coming. The priest asks who:

> JOEY: The demons, the demons!
> PRIEST: Demons? Demons aren't real, they are only parables, metaphors.
> > (*The church door explodes inward, revealing PINHEAD.*)
> JOEY: (*pointing at the demon*) Then what the fuck is that?!

Like the priest in "Good God, Y'all," the priest in *Hellraiser III* is killed by the very demonic

forces that he has spent his entire life preaching about and yet, moments before death, denied

existed. And like the *Supernatural* storyline, his death is quickly passed over in favor of following a larger fight sequence. It is not that we, as the audience, want either of the priests to die, necessarily, but we are also not invested in them as characters so in a sense, we do not care about their deaths. They have proven themselves unimportant to the story through their doubt.

In some cases, it is not that the religious figure seems not to believe in his or her own doctrine, but the fault lies in believing in it too much. These religious characters are so bound by their religious belief that they cannot see when it is being manipulated or the actual truth of that belief. In the episode "99 Problems" (4.17) Sam and Dean stumble upon a small town where the residents have accepted, as a whole, that demons are real and that the apocalypse is coming. Part of their acceptance is practical – there is an inordinate amount of demonic activity happening in the surrounding area that they cannot ignore – so they form demon-hunting militias, and the other part is based on faith in the preacher's daughter, Leah, who is believed to be a prophet of the Lord. The people of the town follow Leah's word like gospel, even when she tells them to kill members of their own community to cleanse them of their sins. In a classic *Supernatural* move, Leah, of course, is not really a prophet but a demon – specifically the whore of Babylon as described in Revelation – come to lead the religious astray. The townsfolk's blind obedience to Leah's orders, no matter how seemingly ridiculous or inhumane, highlights our view of extreme, fundamental believers and, by association, all Christianity.

Specifically in *Supernatural*, we have a variety of characters like the priest from "Good God, Y'all" who do not believe the apocalypse could actually be real or characters who seem to represent faith/religious belief but turn out to be demonic, or at least supernatural, or simply charlatans instead of faithful. Early in the series, in the episode aptly titled "Faith" (1.12) we meet faith-healer Roy LeGrange. Roy seems to be "the real deal," a blind man led by God in "choosing who to heal by helping [him] see into people's hearts." When Dean is brought onto the stage with Roy, he expresses doubt, explaining that he does not believe in Roy's abilities – "I'm not a believer." Roy smiles as he drops a hand on Dean's head and says, "You will be, son. You will be." He "lays hands" on Dean and, along with a prayer, heals the heart damage Dean received earlier via electric shock while killing a demon. It all seems miraculous and awe-inspiring, and Roy seems to genuinely feel he has been given a gift from God.

The reality is that Roy had no gift. His wife had turned to dark magic to save his life when he developed cancer and she figured out a spell to bind a reaper – a supernatural being responsible for taking souls – and keep it from taking her husband. Roy took his renewed health as a miracle and his wife, Sue Ann, encouraged him to continue. She kept the reaper enslaved as a way to punish those whom she felt were immoral or needed to be punished. She would call the reaper forth with an incantation, blood ritual and Coptic cross and instruct it to take the illness from whomever Roy was "healing" and put it into the body of someone she felt deserved death such as a woman who advocated for abortion rights or a man who was an openly gay school teacher. In the end, Sam and Dean break the spell and the reaper is released and kills Sue Ann, leaving Roy alone and confused as to what happened to his gift.

Within the episode, we track the arc of belief and faith from believing Roy is really healing people to believing Roy is, as Dean says, "playing God … deciding who lives and dies" by controlling a reaper, to realizing that Sue Ann, the preacher's wife who has been so gentle, patient and kind throughout the episode, is actually the one killing people. Like Roy, she proclaims to be doing God's work, but the image of religion and God she puts forth is far from his loving acceptance. She feels justified in her actions, claiming "The Lord chose me to reward the just and punish the wicked. … It is God's will." She's more like a caricature of every right-wing Christian fundamentalist stereotype of organized religion, leading Dean to say, "May God save us from half the people who think they're doing God's work."

This criticism of the organized church by having the faith-healer's wife be corrupt is doubly established by having her turn to dark magic instead of relying on God. When Sam and Dean are figuring out that Sue Ann is responsible, Sam describes how she trapped the reaper:

> SAM: You gotta build a black altar with seriously dark stuff. Bones, human blood… To cross a line like that, a preacher's wife. Black magic. Murder. Evil.
> DEAN: Desperate. Her husband was dying, she didn't have anything to save him.

And yet when Roy describes his miraculous recovery, he references his faith. Roy explains that when he was diagnosed with cancer, he prayed for healing: "I was weak, but I told Sue Ann, 'You just keep right on praying.' I went into a coma. Doctors said I wouldn't wake up, but I did. And the cancer was gone." But Sue Ann had no faith – no trust in God to save her husband, so she made it happen herself. If we go by Dean's words, it is not even that she had no faith in God, but that there isn't a God to help her to begin with – "she didn't have anything to save him." When Sam and Dean are narrowing down that it is a reaper at fault for the deaths, Dean says, "There's only one thing that can give and take life like that – we're dealing with a reaper." There's no mention of God or Christ, two figures in the Christian mythos who are most associated with giving and taking life – nor is there any reference to other deities from various religions. For all intents and purposes, the church is empty of power and its officials are corrupt.

This view of the church is also seen in the episode "Houses of the Holy" (2.13), in which people are being visited by an "angel" who instructs them to kill people who are evil. The first person to be visited explains what the angel spoke to her:

> SAM: And this angel…
> GLORIA: Spoke God's Word.
> SAM: And the Word was to kill someone?
> GLORIA: I know, it sounds strange. But what I did was very important. I helped him smite an evil man. I was chosen. For redemption.
> …
> SAM: Why him?
> GLORIA: I just know what the angel told me: that this man was guilty to his deepest foundations. And that was good enough for me.

When Sam researches the victim, Carl Gully, he does not really see any signs that point to him being evil; specifically, Sam describes Gully as "a churchgoer." Because the entertainment world has taught us that the universe loves irony, this of course foreshadows that Gully will be discovered to have some hidden secret. Before long, Sam and Dean find three bodies buried in his basement – "guilty to his deepest foundations" indeed – that turn out to be three missing college students from the campus library Gully worked at. A second victim of an angel-inspired killer is found out to be a pedophile setting up an online relationship with a 13-year old girl. He is a member of the same church that Gully went to. Once again, we see corruption within the church.

When Sam and Dean explore the church, they discover that a priest, Father Gregory, recently died a violent death on the church steps, making him a prime candidate for being a vengeful spirit going after those who revealed sinful natures and secrets while in confession. Sam does not want to believe that – he would rather believe that God is intervening and answering the prayers for cleansing and help from the young priest, Father Reynolds, still at the church. At the end of the episode, it is proven that it is, in fact, the spirit of Father

Gregory and not an angel or God killing these people. When Father Gregory reveals himself to Father Reynolds he says, "I've come in answer to your prayers" ("Houses of the Holy"). He does not claim to be sent by God, but is active in his choice to come as a spirit of vengeance. There is effectively no power of God here.

When it is revealed in Seasons 4 and 5 that angels do exist, the perception of Christianity is not improved. The angels are not the touchy-feely types seen on *Highway to Heaven* or *Touched by an Angel*. They are inhuman warriors who seldom seem to see the value of humanity. A top angel in the ranks, Zachariah, is constantly dressed in a suit and speaks of the apocalypse and heaven in terms of finance and business. He comes across very much like a fat-cat bureaucrat compared to the blue-collar working stiffs of the rest of the world. Uriel, another angel, calls humans "mud monkeys" and very few of the angels we see ever seem to take the loss of human life hard. They are not here on earth to guide or guard humanity – they are here to shepherd in the apocalypse so that the big fight can be over with. In this is the final betrayal of trust in religious figures. Dean has given himself over to help heaven prevent Lucifer from rising, but instead they are going to hold him until it is his time to become Michael's vessel. From the very source of faith – angels, God, and heaven – we would expect honesty and honest faith. Instead, we get an absent God and angels who lie and kill their own kind in order to reach their own selfish ends. If they are no better than us, than humans, then what hope is there of there being an honest faith experience? Instead, we are left to follow the paths of Sam and Dean – looking out for our own selves and trusting in our own hearts and instincts to guide us while the trappings of organized faith and religion are left behind.

Death and the Value of Human Life

In terms of his teachings and lifestyle, Jesus is not all that different from any number of philosophers. Religiously speaking, what makes him the Christ and the figurehead of Christianity is that he went to the cross, died and then came back to life. He did not merely appear as a spirit; he was not undead, as modern pop culture likes to joke; he was resurrected into his physical body as a living being. Even though Jesus reportedly raised people from the dead on more than a few occasions, the idea of being dead and coming back to life is still impressive.[6] The pain of the death he willingly suffered, the separation from God that taking on the sins of the world brought him, and the subsequent three days spent in the afterlife before returning to the world are what set Christ's sacrifice above those of even other Christian martyrs.

There is some question as to whether Christ was in hell or heaven for the three days of his death. The Apostle's Creed states that Jesus died and "descended into hell," based off the translation of the Hebrew *sheol*, which means afterlife, into the Greek word *hades*, which we have taken to mean Hell. Biblical scholars argue instead that Christ went to paradise based on interpretations of several verses, most notably Christ's response to the thief on the cross when he said that he would be with Him that day in paradise (Luke 23:43). Either way, Christ's sacrifice is ultimate – if he suffered and died and went to hell for the sake of the people of the world, it is an ultimate sacrifice. If he suffered and died, went to paradise and then came back to humanity, it is a sacrifice because he had to give up heaven and return to a world of pain and imperfection. The return to life symbolizes the victory over death because

---

[6] Jesus raised the widow's son at Nain (Luke 7:11-17), Lazarus (John 11:1-44) and Jairus' daughter (Mark 5:21-43).

when Christ leaves again, he ascends into heaven on a cloud.[7] His physical body is taken to heaven; there is no second physical death because Christ has defeated death.

Most Christ figures do not follow this pattern all the way through the resurrection and return to life because they are meant to be human representations of Christ-like behavior. If they were able to repeat Christ's death and resurrection completely, it would undermine the uniqueness of the very act that makes Christ special to Christianity. As time has progressed and we have developed a more thorough understanding of biology and medicine, Christ figures have been able to have closer encounters of death such as comas or out-of-body experiences, or perhaps technical/scientific death followed by a resurrection due to outside involvement – like Buffy receiving CPR after her first death in "Prophecy Girl" (1.12). If these figures do manage to survive their death/sacrifice, it is seen as miraculous or special – they are unique. And rarely do we see these figures commit the same acts of death and sacrifice more than once.[8] The uniquity of death and resurrection is still important.

With *Supernatural*, however, the death of main characters is quite frequent, as is their resurrection. Within the first five seasons, Sam dies three times, Castiel dies twice, and Dean dies over one hundred times.[9] Death and coming back to life after death is nothing new for the characters of *Supernatural*, so much so that fans of the show do not really question *if* a character is actually going to die, but at what point and in what way the writers will work to

---

[7] See Mark 16:19-20, Luke 24:36-53, Acts 1:6-12 and 1 Timothy 3:16.

[8] Buffy dies twice – once in "Prophecy Girl" and once in "The Gift" (5.22) and is brought back to life both times. It can be argued that she technically dies three times, however. In "The Wish" (3.9) Cordelia makes a wish that transports us to an alternate dimension where Buffy is the Slayer based out of Cincinnati. When she comes to battle the Master in Sunnydale, she is killed in the battle. So while she technically dies without a resurrection (that we know of, since we never go to that dimension again), it is not the same Buffy that we follow throughout the series, so I argue that this death does not count for the series.

[9] Sam dies in the episodes: "All Hell Breaks Loose, Part II" (2.22), "Dark Side of the Moon" (5.16) and "Swan Song" (5.22); Castiel dies in the episodes: "Lucifer Rising" (4.22) and "Swan Song" (5.22); Dean dies once each in "No Rest for the Wicked" (3.16) and "Dark Side of the Moon" (5.16), but in "The Mystery Spot" (3.11), he dies over a hundred different times while trapped in a time loop by the Trickster/Gabriel.

bring him back. While it is true that not all of these character deaths are moments of Christly sacrifice, the commonness of death and resurrection does have an effect on how we value the sacrificial deaths. The first few times a character dies for another, as a specific act of sacrifice and exchange, are heartbreaking. John, Sam and Dean's father, makes a deal with the demon he has been hunting his whole life to spare Dean's life and take John in his place in "In My Time of Dying" (2.1). At the end of that season, Dean repeats his father's actions by making a deal with a Crossroad Demon in order to bring Sam back to life after a fatal stab wound ("All Hell Breaks Loose, Parts I & II" 2.21-2.22). At the end of Season 3, when we expect Sam, Dean and fellow hunter and father-figure Bobby to figure out a way to kill the head demon Lilith and free Dean from his deal, Dean is ripped to shreds by hellhounds and his soul is taken to Hell where we see him strung out on chains and meathooks in a crucifix position, screaming out Sam's name.

Executive Producer and director Kim Manners (who also worked on *The X-Files*) said circumventing expectation and actually sending Dean to Hell was "definitely the right thing to do" because if "he'd weaseled his way out of it somehow, it would've been a big letdown to the story. He had to pay the piper" (Knight, *The Official Companion: Season 3* 96). To some extent, Manners is right. If Dean was not made to make good on his deal, then the sacrifice he made to bring Sam back loses some of its impact, especially considering how the entire season has been focused on the ramifications of Dean's deal and how to break it so he would not have to die. For Dean, family is all important – there is nothing he has that is more important. So when Sam is dead, Dean wastes no time considering his options and immediately offers the one thing he has that he feels is a worthy trade, even taking the paltry deal of one year for his soul instead of the usual ten years that most Crossroad Demons offer

(Garvey 94). Dean's willingness to die for Sam is equally important because we see throughout Season 2 just how much of an effect John's sacrifice for him had on Dean. Dean's reactions to finding out that John died in his place are reminiscent of our own uncomfortableness with the idea of owing someone for our salvation. He feels unworthy, a feeling that will be repeated when Castiel pulls him from Hell at the beginning of Season 4 in "Lazarus Rising" (4.1). Even knowing how that debt will hang on Sam, Dean cannot allow his brother to die when he can do something, anything, to prevent it.

When it comes time for Dean to die at the end of Season 3, he makes Sam promise not to do anything rash – like make a deal with a demon – to get him out of Hell because that would just put them right back where they started: dying for each other. Sam and Dean have the type of brotherly love and familial bond that only comes from severe tragedy and being responsible for one another's well-being; it is the type of bond that most families can only ever dream of sharing, and yet it frequently gets them killed (Wilson x, xiv). In the meta-episode, "The Real Ghostbusters" (5.9),[10] which deals with fan-culture, one fan of the *Supernatural* book series says, "Alright, look, in real life, he sells stereo equipment, I fix copiers. *Our* lives suck. But to be Sam and Dean – to wake up every morning and save the world, to have a brother who would *die* for you... Well, who *wouldn't* want that?" Dean answers, "Well, maybe you've got a point," and the fan does. We all want to think our lives

---

[10] *Supernatural* has made new strides in the idea of meta-stories, starting in Season 4 with "The Monster at the End of This Book" in which we meet Chuck Shirley, a prophet of the Lord and hack writer who has been writing down the adventures of Sam and Dean as a sci-fi/horror novel series not realizing that the images he was getting were divine prophecies. Also called the Winchester Gospels, the books detailed every moment of the boys' lives up through Dean dying and going to Hell. The show used the storyline to comment on its relationship with the fans. Then, in Season 5, Chuck returned, having been writing/publishing more novels. Sam and Dean find him at a fan convention for the *Supernatural* novel series where they meet and interact with LARP-ing (Live Action Role Play) fans who are dressed and acting like Sam and Dean. This meta-line extends even farther in "The French Mistake" (6.15) where Sam and Dean are sent to an alternate dimension where they are Jared Padalecki and Jensen Ackles (the actors who actually play the characters in the show) and *Supernatural* is a TV show.

are that important, that epic; that what we do has an impact on the world. We all want that level of dedication, to know that someone loves and cares for us so much that they *would* do anything. The danger comes when that person actually *acts*, when it is not just an empty "I would die for you," but a fulfilled, "I *died* for you," (and not just "died" but "died and went to Hell to suffer for 30, 40, 100 years") that we begin to see a problem. That type of debt can never be fully repaid and leaves us feeling somewhat resentful of owing it.

The act of death and dying, then, is not new to *Supernatural*. In fact, the death of the main characters is almost expected at this point. In Season 5, as the apocalypse approaches, Death personified even becomes a recurring character, first appearing in "Two Minutes to Midnight" (5.21). But this is not merely the Grim Reaper come to collect the souls of the dead – those characters, Reapers, make an appearance in the first season episode "Faith" (1.6) and work in service of Death. This is Death, one of the four horsemen of the apocalypse as foretold in Revelation. Death, as a character, is tall, sallow and somber, with black hair and a long, black coat – as we would expect Death to be in a modern world, perhaps. He even carries a scythe. But this is *Supernatural*, so expectations are not entirely the norm. Instead of meeting Death in a graveyard or perhaps even a church or morgue, we first see him exiting a 1960s-era white Cadillac with a vanity plate that reads "BUH*BYE" ("Two Minutes to Midnight"). During a slow camera pan of Death walking down a street to Jennifer Titus' rendition of "O Death," a rude man on a cell phone bumps into him and snipes at him. Death walks by and casually brushes his shoulder; behind him, we see the rude man suddenly drop dead on the sidewalk. This is Death.

The whole reason the horseman Death is manifested is because Lucifer has performed a spell to bind Death to him and basically force him to participate in the upcoming apocalypse. This sets Death up as an enemy to be fought for Sam and Dean who are both

fighting to stop the apocalypse. This is not new territory for *Supernatural*. Death, as in the

act of dying or losing life, is one of the key opponents the Winchesters face throughout the

series. In the second episode of the series, "Wendigo," Dean explains that their absent father

gave them his journal, what Dean identifies as John's "single most valuable possession,"

because he wants Sam and Dean to "pick up where he left off. You know, saving people,

hunting things. The family business" ("Wendigo"). It is their job, as it were, to keep people

from dying at the claws, teeth or ectoplasm-coated spirit fingers, of as many "evil sons of

bitches" as possible. It is not that the Winchesters do not understand that death is a part of

life, especially their lives, but they are trying to give people as much of a chance to die

naturally instead of supernaturally. They are living examples of what happens when

supernatural death touches people, and so they try to prevent it from happening to others. In

"What Is and What Should Never Be" (2.20), we see a world in which Sam and Dean were

not affected by demons; they never went out as hunters and, as a result, hundreds of people

died premature, unnatural deaths. Because of their intervention, families remained whole and

lives progressed naturally (Hannah-Jones 62).

This type of salvation from untimely death is extended to anyone threatened by

supernatural forces. Sam and Dean do not discriminate on who should or should not be

saved. In "Folsom Prison Blues" (2.19), the Winchesters let themselves be arrested and sent

to prison in order to protect the prisoners from a vengeful spirit. They have been called in by

the warden, an old friend of their father's. Sam scoffs at Dean's insistence that they are here

to save "innocent people," to which Dean replies, "just because these people are in jail,

doesn't mean they deserve to die. If we don't stop this thing, people are going to continue to die. We do this job wherever it takes us" ("Folsom Prison Blues"). They are not there to protect the prison guards – the spirit only goes after the prisoners – but the prisoners, even the ones on death row who will die soon anyway. Dean accepts that they should be in jail and is not advocating a repeal of the death penalty, although he does make a crack about Sam's attitude towards the prisoners as being like that of death-penalty-happy Texas. But he does not believe anyone should be subject to the type of death offered by this spirit. In this episode, we are also reminded of Christ's offer of salvation to the prisoners hanging beside him on Calvary. One of the thieves asks Jesus to remember him and Christ replies, "Truly I say to you, today you shall be with Me in Paradise" (Luke 23:42-43).

This is not the only time that Sam and Dean will venture into an institution to save people from supernatural deaths. In "Sam, Interrupted" (5.11), Sam and Dean basically get themselves checked into an asylum in order to stop whatever is killing patients. Where Dean had to all but drag Sam to jail to protect prisoners on the say-so of their father's friend, this time it is Sam who convinces Dean to check themselves in on the word of Martin, a former hunter who is a patient at the asylum. When they are admitted, Dean meets his psychiatrist, Dr. Cartwright, who classifies him as a "paranoid schizo with narcissistic and religious psychosis" ("Sam, Interrupted"). In order to get admitted, Sam and Dean basically told the truth about what they do – hunting demons and trying to stop Lucifer from bringing on the apocalypse – which immediately prompted them being committed. It is interesting to note that we deem their story as a sign of insanity when put against the context of "reality."

This idea of lunacy is often joked about on *Supernatural*, with Dean expressing it outright during a rant about how he and Sam specifically go out looking for monsters and demons and things that want to kill them. "You know who does that?" he asks, "Crazy people!" ("Yellow Fever" 4.6). For a brief moment in "Sam, Interrupted," we get to see how the outside world of "reality" views the level of belief and almost religious fervor that Sam and Dean have for "the family business." We treat people the same if they believe themselves to be the reincarnation of Napoleon Bonaparte or Christ, himself. From the view of the show, where Sam and Dean are telling the truth, it is amusing that they are considered crazy. But from the outside reality where we know monsters and demons do not exist, it is easy to see how we instantly categorize this type of belief or faith as being "out there." One cannot help but wonder what we would do with Christ today. Would we label Christ, the self-proclaimed "way, the truth and the life," as a "paranoid schizo with narcissistic and religious psychosis?" Because organized religion has achieved such a negative connotation both in the realm of *Supernatural* and outside it, it would not be too much of a stretch to believe that, were we to meet Christ face to face today, we would automatically assume him to be a loony and lock him away.

"Sam, Interrupted" also shows us a look into Dean's headspace regarding his role as a savior. Up until the fourth and fifth season, Dean has seen his job as being fairly limited – take out the bad guys, save the random, innocent individual from a gruesome, untimely death, and move on to the next – but now he is acknowledging the scale in which he finds himself. It is, literally, apocalyptic. Dr. Cartwright asks why it has to be Dean fighting the monsters instead of someone else, to which Dean self-deprecatingly replies that he "Can't find anybody else that dumb," before simply saying "It's my job. Somebody's gotta save people's asses." Cartwright's questioning of why it has to be Dean mimics Dean's own thoughts from earlier in the series. In "What Is and What Should Never Be" (2.20), after fighting a djinn (a genie-type creature), Dean finds himself in an alternate reality where he and Sam never became hunters. His mother was not killed by demon fire and his father did not have to sacrifice himself to save Dean's life but rather died of natural causes after living a full, happy life. But Dean keeps getting flashes of people in trouble in reality – ones that will die if he does not return there. So Dean finds himself at his father's grave, asking why he, Dean, should be required to give up this existence to save anyone:

> DEAN: All of them. Everyone that you saved, everyone Sammy and I saved. They're all dead. … It's like my old life is, is coming after me or something. Like it doesn't want me to be happy. Course I know what you'd say. … "So go hunt the djinn. He put you here, it can put you back. Your happiness for all those people's lives, no contest. Right?" But why? Why is it my job to save these people? Why do I have to be some kind of hero? What about us, huh? What, Mom's not supposed to live her life, Sammy's not supposed to get married? Why do we have to sacrifice everything, Dad?

In this moment, we see in Dean's questioning an echo of Jesus in the Garden at Gethsemane before his arrest in the Gospels of Matthew and Luke. In Matthew 26, starting in verse 36, Jesus goes to the Garden of Gethsemane to pray about the upcoming crucifixion. He tells the apostles with him, "My soul is deeply grieved, to the point of death" (Matthew 26:38). When he goes deeper into the garden, he falls on his face and prays, "My Father, if it is possible, let this cup pass from Me: yet not as I will, but as You will" (Matthew 26:39). He repeats this prayer three separate times, begging not to have to fulfill his role as savior if there is any other way. The Gospel of Luke goes so far as to describe this scene as an ordeal of agony, saying that Jesus prayed so fervently that "His sweat became like drops of blood, falling down upon the ground" (Luke 22:44).

In the end, both Jesus and Dean follow the will of their fathers and sacrifice themselves for the good of others. In the case of Christ, this means the absolving of sin. For Dean, it is simply saving another life at the cost of his own. In order to escape the dream world the djinn put him in, Dean must kill himself, effectively killing the happy "lives" of his family that existed there as well. But he does save the other victims of the djinn, and Sam. He still questions the amount they are asked to give, however, telling Sam, "all I can think about is how much this job has cost us. We've lost so much… We've sacrificed so much." Sam is quick to reply that it is worth the sacrifice because "people are alive because of you [Dean]." Sam asserts, "It's worth it, Dean. It is," though he does admit that "It's not fair, and y'know, it hurts like hell, but it's worth it." ("What Is and What Should Never Be"). Life is restored and death is defeated, so it is worth it.

By the time of "Sam, Interrupted," however, the scales have changed. It is not merely one life or even a community on the line as the Winchesters have dealt with before. Instead, it is the entire world. Cartwright asks if there's a quota of people Dean has to save, and Dean replies that he has to save "all of them" ("Sam, Interrupted"). Dean is not speaking of salvation in the religious sense – he has no plans for their souls – but the physical salvation of life from the impending death and destruction of the apocalypse. Cartwright's phrasing of the question is interesting to consider here – "So, is there a quota? How many people do you have to save?" On one hand, it could be looked at as a discussion of "how many lives are on the line," but because of the inclusion of the "quota" line, it comes across more like a goal or a qualification Dean has to fill. He *has to* save so many people in order to… find forgiveness? Be accepted? For Cartwright, looking for a rationalization for Dean's apparent psychosis, this would make sense – he has to save so many in order to escape whatever has brought on this mental snap. But for Dean, it is simply a matter of not letting death (or in this case Lucifer and Death) win:

DEAN: It's the end of the world, okay? I mean, it's a damn biblical
    apocalypse, and if I don't stop it and save everyone, then no one will,
    and we all die.
CARTWRIGHT: That's horrible.
DEAN: Yeah, tell me about it.
CARTWRIGHT: I mean, apocalypse or no apocalypse… monsters or no
    monsters, that's a crushing weight to have on your
    shoulders. To feel like six billion lives depend on you.
    God… how do you get up in the morning?
DEAN: That's a good question.

Dean's entire rationalization for his actions is to stop the death of everyone in the world. It is not a question of saving souls or converting people to a belief or even defeating Lucifer as a servant of God. In fact, Dean is fairly vocal in how he views God, the heavenly authority, and his angels, and that view is not positive. He frequently refers to angels as "dicks" and calls God "just another deadbeat dad with a bunch of excuses" ("Dark Side of the Moon" 5.16). Even before having personal experience with religious figures like Lucifer and God, Dean was not motivated in his actions by religion. He never had faith in God or Heaven, claiming: "There's no higher power, there's no God. I mean, there's just chaos, and violence, and random unpredictable evil that comes out of nowhere, and rips you to shreds" ("Houses of the Holy" 2.13). When it becomes rather clear that not only is there a God but that he is responsible for sending an angel, Castiel, to save Dean from Hell, Dean still has problems with the idea of God existing and there still being evil in the world: "If he doesn't exist, fine. Bad crap happens to good people. That's how it is. … I can roll with that. But if he is out there, what's wrong with him? Where the hell is he while all these decent people are getting torn to shreds? … You know, why doesn't he help?" ("Are You There, God? It's Me, Dean Winchester" 4.2).

Dean understands a certain, almost karmic balance in the world, saying that he figured the fact that he had "saved some people" made up for the drinking, stealing and other socially negative aspects of his existence. But he did not save them to get on God's good side, nor does he understand why such actions would make God interested in him. He works to save peoples' lives because that is his job, "the family business," and thanks to his father, he is good at it. In "We've Got Work to Do: Sacrifice, Heroism, and Sam and Dean Winchester," Amy Garvey questions whether this, Dean's life as a hunter and how he saves lives, actually make him heroic. She asks, "Is he [Dean] really a hero if he believes the only thing he's good for is aiming a shotgun full of rock salt and burning bones?" (92). While it is true that Dean has never really known any other life than that of being a hunter, I think this goes back to Kawal's arguments of saintly and heroic actions. He is not merely stuck fighting demons. He could choose to settle down and protect his own family from the supernatural rather than traveling the country and looking for problems to fix. Even if Dean feels no fear for himself in these situations or stops to question his role in them, his actions still serve as heroic moments of salvation. There is large difference between feeling only suited to one line of work or existence, as it were, and dedicating one's life solely to that existence. Dean may feel only good for taking down supernatural baddies, but that does not require him to sacrifice himself for the whole world.

So regardless of their acts of salvation and sacrifice, neither Sam nor Dean are acting out of any connection to or desire to please God. God is not part of their plans, even after he, heaven, and angels are introduced into the show's canon in Season 4, leaving what Gregory Stevenson called a "rather one-sided view of the supernatural" in his essay "Horror, Humanity, and the Demon in the Mirror" (42). For Stevenson, this dearth of benevolent beings equally powerful to the demons and dark forces being contended with left *Supernatural*'s focus on the human struggle "between the good and evil impulses within ourselves" (42). Series creator Eric Kripke echoes this sentiment when explaining why there was a strict "no angel policy" for the first three seasons of the series. "I had this notion in my head," Kripke says, "that the only forces of good in the universe were humans, and that it was sweaty, disheveled, confused humans up against this overwhelming supernatural threat. … I didn't want massive supernatural creatures … to come in and save them" (Knight, *Official Companion, Season 4* 8). Some critics see Sam and Dean filling this void of strong, positive forces. Writing prior to the appearance of angels in Season 4, Avril Hannah-Jones argues in her essay, "Good and Evil in the World of *Supernatural*" that Sam and Dean function as angels themselves. When they appear in times and places of trouble, they are similar to early biblical angels, "warriors in human guise" described in various scriptures (62).[11] Whether they are serving as the representatives of humanity or angelic forces, however, Sam and Dean are more concerned with the safety and protection of human life than fulfilling any religious function.

God and angels in *Supernatural* have never really been concerned about the salvation of human life. When Dean speaks to Castiel in "Are You There God? It's Me, Dean Winchester" (5.2), Castiel explains that angels are back on earth for the first time since the time of Christ to "stop Lucifer." Everything in Castiel's discussion, and almost all the angels who discuss it throughout the rest of the season, is focused on stopping Lucifer, on keeping him in hell. There is no mention of saving or protecting human life. In fact, instead of showing remorse for the loss of over 20 hunters, Castiel is more upset by the loss of six of his angel brethren. He tells Dean that "there's a bigger picture" than humanity. This seeming disregard also appears in a later episode, "It's the Great Pumpkin, Sam Winchester" (4.7). In

---

[11] See Genesis 18, Numbers 22:22-35, and Judges 6:11-24

order to prevent the raising of Samhain by a witch, which is one of the 66 seals that need to

be broken to free Lucifer, Castiel and another angel, Uriel, come to kill the witch by

eradicating the entire town she is hiding in. Castiel calls it "regrettable" that over one

thousand people must be killed, but says it is ordained by heaven, and therefore just, to

prevent the rise of both Samhain and, eventually, Lucifer.

While the argument can be made that in stopping Lucifer and the apocalypse, the

angels are saving the lives of everyone on the planet, it is in the intentions and small actions

that we see their lack of value for human life. Given the choice of leaving so Castiel and

Uriel can smite the town and Samhain or staying and attempting to kill the witch and save the

town, Sam and Dean do not even hesitate to stay. They refuse to leave and Dean even

threatens to fight removal so hard that Uriel will have to kill him anyway in order to prevent

the needless deaths of the townspeople. In the end, Sam and Dean fail to prevent the rise of

Samhain, but they do kill him and save the town, so there is a sense of victory. However,

they are, as Castiel says, now one step closer to having hell on earth should Lucifer rise.

Castiel also reveals that his and Uriel's orders were not to destroy the town but to do

whatever Dean said. It was a test; whether Dean passed or failed is unknown. For Castiel,

who sees humanity as God's creations – as "works of art" – and has begun to doubt the

justness of his heavenly mission, Dean passed because he chose to work for humanity. For

Uriel, who repeatedly calls Sam and Dean "mud-monkeys" and has almost no fondness for

humanity, this was not a triumph.

As the series progresses, it is revealed that the angels have been giving themselves

orders. God is mysteriously absent and so the angels have decided to hasten the apocalypse.

Instead of waiting for some grand battle that they are sure they will win (after all, the ending is already spoiled in Revelation), they decide to cease their attempts to stop Lucifer and instead welcome his arrival. Castiel breaks from heaven and the ranks of the angels and joins with Sam and Dean to try and return Lucifer to hell and stop the full-blown apocalypse. Castiel's major plan of attack is to find God and get him involved in the battle. When Dean scoffs at the idea, Castiel assures him that the move is "not a theological issue. It's strategic" ("Good God Y'all" 5.2). Even Castiel, an angel, has no misgivings about the merciful or saving grace of God in the world of *Supernatural*. Should God desire to save humanity, Castiel would not need to go find him. Instead, he is going to search out an ally, to convince him to join the fight. All of Castiel's searching is for naught, however. In "Dark Side of the Moon" (5.16), we meet Joshua, an angel and caretaker of the garden in heaven who is said to be in direct contact with God. Joshua explains that God is on Earth and aware of the situation but has no plans to intervene, preferring to let mankind exercise the free will he gave them upon their creation. He has already intervened in rescuing Sam and Dean from Lucifer's gate and bringing Castiel back to life; he has no plans to get further involved.

For Erin Giannini in her article, "There's nothing more dangerous than some a-hole who thinks he's on a holy mission: Using and (Dis) Abusing Religious and Economic Authority on *Supernatural*," this policy of non-involvement shows how Supernatural works to "repackage" religion (174). The existence of God is confirmed while at the same time the omnipotent power of the Christian God is questioned (174). For Giannini and other critics, this type of repackaging is evidence that *Supernatural* is not focused on one specific religion, like Christianity. I argue, however, that this type of presence and absence is seen throughout *Supernatural*, especially in the early seasons before Christianity became canon. Dean openly mocks a faith in God, yet he and Sam still make use of crosses, holy water, Christian exorcism rites and the name of God/Christ to identify demons. There is a sense of faith in the power of the relic existing outside a faith in what gives the relic its power in the first place. To a certain extent, this is an example of Ziolkowski's idea of the cultural possession of the Gospels. Faith is not necessary for them to have a specific power. But even more so, *Supernatural* establishes Christianity as the most potent/powerful religion without officially evoking it. Where *Buffy* made use of crosses and holy water simply because that was the established lore for killing vampires, *Supernatural* invokes the name of Christ and Christian exorcism rituals as a method of identifying and defeating all demons of all faiths and cultures, not just those connected to Lucifer.[12] So in *Supernatural*, we seem to have a functioning faith in the power of the name of Christ without religious faith/belief in the actual existence of the deity being invoked.

This religion-less faith is seen time and time again in Dean's interactions with Castiel as he works to save humanity. Dean has no desire to conform or be converted to the beliefs of the angels, but he is drawn to the emerging spark of humanity that he sees in Castiel. When Dean is fighting to escape the angels at the end of Season 4, he needs Castiel's help to do so. The way that Dean appeals to Castiel is through human emotions and contacts; he references family and compares heaven and the angels to soulless, faceless bosses and company bureaucrats. He even humanizes Castiel by repeatedly addressing him by a nickname – Cass. In the end, Castiel does help, but they are too late to prevent the last seal breaking and the rise of Lucifer. So now, they can only band together to attempt to put him back in Hell and stop the apocalypse.

---

[12] In "Phantom Traveler" (1.4), Sam and Dean take on a demon from an unspecified Asian religion/culture, and yet the demon flinches and responds to the name of God/Christ (Cristo) being spoken at it, being doused in holy water and the exorcism ritual.

In Christian terms, the apocalypse is a battle already won, with Christ leading the armies of heaven to defeat Lucifer and bring forth a new heaven on earth. For *Supernatural*, however, this is not a foregone conclusion, and even if heaven wins, humanity is not guaranteed a paradise. In "Lucifer Rising" (5.1), the angels tell Dean that they are fully prepared to lose upwards of ten million human lives in the battle against Lucifer. Their excuse is that it is to save the billions of the planet, but it still seems harsh and inconceivable. When Sam asks Bobby, the Winchester's fellow hunter and father-figure, what they can do, he does not speak in apocalyptic terms, but keeps it at a human, individual level, saying, "We save as many as we can for as long as we can, I guess. It's bad. Whoever wins, Heaven or Hell, we're boned." In a taste of the type of conviction Dean will come to later in the season, he responds: "What if we win? I'm serious. Screw the angels and the demons and their crap apocalypse. Now they wanna fight a war, let them get their own planet. This one's ours and I say they get the hell off it. We take 'em all on. We kill the Devil, hell we even kill Michael, but we do it our own damned selves" ("Lucifer Rising"). Dean pulls back into his humanity rather than embrace the power of the angels and their offer to defeat Lucifer if Dean allows the archangel Michael to use him as a vessel.

Dean's assertion that this is *our* planet and that we stop the apocalypse "*our* own damned selves" reveals a trend in American Christianity to pull away from the organized, formal religion and find our own individual faith. Even though it is established that God created the earth, Dean still claims it as belonging to humans and expresses the urge to kick all religious beings, both good and evil, off it. When Bobby asks how Dean plans to accomplish this lofty goal, Dean eloquently replies, "I got no idea. What I do have is a GED and a give 'em hell attitude. I'll figure it out" ("Lucifer Rising"). This type of individualistic,

brash American heroics is very carefully crafted within *Supernatural*.

As we have already seen, series creator Eric Kripke specifically avoided strong,

powerful forces of good in order for the human struggle to be front and center. Now that

angels and God are in the picture, that sense of humanity and the value of human emotions,

drive and life are more important than ever. "I always loved the idea that you have this very

epic, highfalutin prophecy about chosen ones and end times," Kripke says, "and then you

have this blue-collar guy, who's American and stubborn and cocky, walk up to it and say,

'Prophecy is for wussies. Go to hell!' and kick it in the ass" (Knight, *The Official Guide:

Season 5* 9).[13] For Kripke and the world of *Supernatural*, the human story will always be

compelling, perhaps not necessarily more so than the apocalypse, but in spite of it.

The apocalypse storyline of *Supernatural*, abounds with angels and demons and God

and the Devil, and even the occasional cameo by non-Christian gods,[14] and in the midst of it

all is this group of humans who are trying to stay human despite it all – to not give up and

just let death and inhumanity happen. "There's humanity," Kripke explains of the

apocalypse, "and a bunch of supernatural sons-of-bitches that are screwing with humanity,

and humanity will always win" (Knight, *The Official Guide: Season 5* 10). It is not a question

of religious right or authority, but saving every human life possible; "It's about simple

honesty and the dignity of human nature," Kripke claims before channeling Dean and

---

[13] Throughout Season 5, Dean refers to himself, Sam and Castiel as "Team Free will," because they are fighting back against the predestination of the apocalypse and heaven ("The Song Remains the Same" 5.13). This is reminiscent of the American Individualism concept, which rejected the predestination of Calvinism, exhibited by American authors Ralph Waldo Emerson, Ben Franklin, Walt Whitman and Henry David Thoreau, to name a few.

[14] See "Hammer of the Gods" (5.19) in which a collection of pagan gods, such as Loki, Baldur, Odin and Kali, meet to discuss the Judeo-Christian apocalypse and plan a way to stop it because they are tired of the bickering between Lucifer and Michael.

exclaiming that "All these highfalutin creatures, whether they're angels or demons, can suck it!" (Knight 10).

To a certain extent, this is the utmost example of what our Common Christ figures have become. They are not supernatural figures bent on epic quests to save the world. Instead, the Common Christ is a regular human being who works to save humanity in any way he or she can. The Common Christ does not require faith or belief from those he saves, nor do his actions have eternal consequences. Instead, as Dean displays, he appears when needed, saves as many lives as he can while killing as many evil things as he can, and leaves before too many even know he was even there.

Regardless of whether Sam and Dean are fighting a regular monster-of-the-week or battling Lucifer, Michael and all the angels and demons of the world, the emphasis is constantly placed on the human aspect of the story because that is where the heart of it lies. Human emotion and understanding is what gives *Supernatural* its "ambiguity of evil"; nothing in the *Supernatural*/supernatural landscape is as easily classified and categorized as we would like (Abbott xii). Vampires can be "vegans," angels can be "dicks," demons can be helpful allies, heroes can slip and fall, and death/Death is not always an enemy to be fought. Even when dealing with metaphysical concept of Death claiming to be as old as God and that when God dies, Death will reap him, too, the story is grounded in human time and experience, allowing Dean to respond to that bit of news that the entire situation is simply "above [his] pay grade" ("Two Minutes to Midnight" 5.21) (Lavery 246). There is never a moment when the death of a human is deemed acceptable, even in spite of the grand scale of the storyline.

In "The End," (5.4) the angel Zachariah gives Dean a glimpse at the future should

Lucifer be allowed to complete his apocalyptic plans. It involves a destroyed civilization with

pockets of fighters and survivors surrounded by zombie-like, demon-infested hordes. More

importantly, it includes Future-Dean who has become incredibly hardened and tough – even

more so than Dean normally is on a good day, which is saying something – and a Fallen-

Angel Castiel who is mortal now and has given himself over to drugs and debauchery.

Present-Dean and Future-Dean plan an assault to kill the Devil once and for all, taking

Castiel and several other members of the compound to help. When they get to the meeting

point, however, Present-Dean realizes that there is no way for the plan to succeed. When he

confronts his future self, Future-Dean admits that the others are there merely as a distraction.

This battle strategy is something Present-Dean, with his value for human life, cannot

understand. He says to his future self, "Oh, man, something is broken in you. You're making

decisions that I would never make. I wouldn't sacrifice my friends," which Future-Dean

agrees with, saying, "You're right. You wouldn't. It's one of the main reasons we're in this

mess, actually" ("The End"). Previously, the two Deans argued over whether Present-Dean

should say yes, let Michael use him as a vessel and kill Lucifer before the apocalypse gets in

full swing:

> FUTURE-DEAN: Well, when you get back home - you say 'yes.' You hear
> me? Say 'yes' to Michael.
> PRESENT-DEAN: That's crazy. If I let him in, then Michael fights the devil.
> The battle's gonna torch half the planet.
> FUTURE-DEAN: Look around you, man. Half the planet's better than no
> planet, which is what we have now. If I could do it over
> again, I'd say 'yes' in a heartbeat.
>
> …
>
> PRESENT-DEAN: Oh, no. There's got to be another way.
> FUTURE-DEAN: Yeah, that's what I thought. I was cocky. Never actually
> thought I'd lose. But I was wrong. Dean. I was wrong. I'm

begging you. Say yes… But you won't. Cause I didn't. Because that's just not us, is it?

This transformation of Dean into one willing to kill billions is hard to take. Future-Dean acknowledges that it is just not his nature back in the present timeline. For us, as well as for Dean, "the thought that anyone needs to die for the 'greater good' is stomach-turning" (Berner 231). In the end, Dean has to make the choice to let someone die, but it is not through him saying yes to Michael. It is in allowing Sam to carry out a plan in which he says yes to Lucifer, allows him inside, and then willingly jumps into Hell in order to trap them both in Hell. Sam makes the sacrifice of his life and soul in Hell to save the world from the apocalypse. Dean sacrifices his brother, promising not to try and resurrect him for fear of resurrecting Lucifer too. This is something we have already seen that Dean is willing to do, so in promising to let Sam stay dead, he is actually sacrificing more than he did previously by being willing to die to bring him back. Instead, Dean is left wishing he had died instead of Sam, or at the very least with him ("Swan Song" 5.22). Dean asks a newly resurrected Castiel (it would appear that God intervened one last time to return him to full-angel fighting force), "What about Sam? What about me, huh? Where's my grand prize? All I got is my brother in a hole!" To which Castiel responds, "You got what you asked for, Dean. No paradise. No hell. Just more of the same. I mean it, Dean. What would you rather have? Peace or Freedom?" ("Swan Song").

It is hard to consider that the two have to be separate, but in the realm of humanity verses the supernatural, peace means giving into the powers of good (or evil) and not fighting anymore, whereas freedom means the possibility of fighting, blood, and death. In the last few scenes of the Season 5 finale "Swan Song," Chuck is seen putting the final touches on the last gospel, the story we have just witnessed in the episode. He does a voice-over of various scenes of Sam and Dean throughout the last five seasons. Chuck says that this has been a test of Sam and Dean, and that they did "all right." "Up against good, evil, angels, devils, destiny, and God himself," Chuck says, "they made their own choice. They chose family. And, well, isn't that kinda the whole point?" ("Swan Song"). Each time, Sam and Dean chose family, chose humanity, chose the independent, individual path separate from what was expected, and in so doing, they saved the world.

When the time for the major battle to unleash the apocalypse comes between Lucifer and Michael (currently residing in Sam and his half-brother Adam, respectively) in "Swan Song," Dean casually drives the Impala onto the battleground of Stull Cemetery in Lawrence, Kansas – the city were it all began so long ago. He does not come to stop the confrontation between Lucifer and Michael, but in a move similar to Xander joining Dark Willow as she attempts to end the world, Dean has come simply to be with Sam at the end of it all, regardless of the outcome (Abbott x). We have followed right along with Dean and Sam throughout this journey and so when the moment comes that Sam gains control of himself again and realizes that he can stop the apocalypse and trap Lucifer, we expect nothing less than for him to throw himself into Hell. He and Dean have long established themselves as sacrificial figures, willing to put themselves in between innocents and harm's way. And they have long since proven that there is nothing they will not do for each other, so when Sam becomes himself again and sees the bloody, battered face of his brother, he knows what he has to do. He spreads his arms out in a crucifix position and falls backward, down into the open pit of Hell, taking Lucifer with him. And then the apocalypse is over.

At least until next season.

Death, Where Is Thy Sting?[15]

Back in "Sam, Interrupted," Dean tells his psychiatrist that he has to keep working because "People are dying," to which Dr. Cartwright replies, "People die all the time." It is a natural progression of life, and when death is natural, Sam and Dean mourn and grieve, but they do not fight it. They focus on fighting the supernatural elements of death, understanding that this could very well mean their own deaths. Early on in the first season, when Dean is electrocuted while fighting a demon and does irreparable damage to his heart, he accepts his fate by saying, "it's a dangerous gig. I drew the short straw" ("Faith" 1.12). Sam, of course, figures out a way to save Dean because that is what the brothers do for each other. They fight death and they fight Death and they refuse to let one another go. There are several times when it seems that Dean would be happy to go, both before and after his time spent in Hell. As he explains, "I'm tired, Sam. I'm tired of this job, this life… of this weight on my shoulders, man. I'm tired of it" ("Croatoan" 2.9).

Writer and Executive Producer Ben Edlund says, "It's a terrible thing when nobody lets you die. They might imprison you forever or take over your body or they might torture you, but you can't get out of the game. That's Sam and Dean's problem" (Lavery 249). This is the same issue we saw with Buffy's resurrection in Season 6. She was dead and at peace and her friends would not let her stay dead. Likewise, Sam and Dean just cannot seem to die. Even with Sam throwing himself into Hell in "Swan Song," as we pan away from Dean at an old girlfriend's house at the very end of the episode, the camera does a slow body shot to reveal someone standing under a streetlight watching – it is Sam. Dean at least stayed in Hell over the three month break between seasons; Sam is back in less than ten minutes.

---

[15] 1 Corinthians 15:55

In terms of Christianity, everlasting life is the gift that Christ offers for our faith and one that he purchased by going to the cross. But how much of a gift is it in terms of our Common Christs? For Sam and Dean, there is no rest, no break. It is not the everlasting life in paradise, but "more of the same" old life on earth ("Swan Song"). In *Supernatural*, we see a very human interpretation of what everlasting life could mean and the harsh realities of being a hero and a figure of salvation. As Chuck says before disappearing at the end of "Swan Song," "No doubt – endings are hard. But then again… nothing ever really ends, does it?" For Sam and Dean, death and resurrection are no longer miraculous. The option of death and triumphant return does not really exist for them. They return, but it is not triumphant and it is not a change from anything.

Though the act of dying in sacrifice may have become common, it still means something to the characters themselves. They are willingly sacrificing their bodies and their lives for humanity, be it one person at a time or the whole world. Even though the act of dying may not seem so difficult, the pain and suffering that always accompanies these deaths gives them the grandness and scale necessary to put them on the same level as Christ's crucifixion and truly establish them as figures of salvation, but unlike Christ, they are ones we can relate to and possibly repay with a bottle of whiskey, a tank of gas and a place to sleep before they head off down the road.

Conclusion: What's the Point? Textual Religion and Self-Salvation

Fakelore, Television Folklore and Textual Religion

The X-Files, *Buffy* and *Supernatural,* to various extents, often rely on folklore as a

plot point. Sometimes, the folklore is used to explain a phenomenon or to offer advice on

how to approach a situation or destroy a monster or a demon. Sometimes, it becomes the

foundation for a belief or a justification for an action. Folklore also has various

representations within each series. For *The X-Files*, lore is represented by the multitude of

files and filing cabinets in Mulder's office. Throughout the seasons, we often see him or

Scully looking into the files for some type of explanation or correlation to the current case. In

Buffy, the lore is the legend of the Slayer herself surrounded by traditional vampire lore.

Giles' books serves much of the same function as Mulder's files to provide explanation and

exposition. Finally, with *Supernatural*, we have John's journal as the portable version of the

library or filing cabinets, along with the books of lore found in Bobby's house and, more

often than not, the frequent visits to actual, local libraries. *Buffy* and *Supernatural* also have a

secondary folklore, or perhaps more to the point, a pop culture lore, in that they often

recognize, point out and comment on popular versions of folklore as comparisons to their

own "real" versions. This works to establish a sense of truth for their lore that *The X-Files*

attains by sheer volume of files and the notion that Mulder is searching for "the truth."

Coming after *The X-Files*, *Buffy* and *Supernatural* also have the added benefit of

including the pop culture attraction of *The X-Files* into their own folklore. Buffy name-drops

Scully in one episode because Giles doubts her: "I cannot believe that you, of all people, are

trying to Scully me. There is something supernatural at work here. Get your books! Look

stuff up!" ("The Pack" 1.6). In this line, Buffy not only establishes her "reality" as being similar to ours because she watches/references *The X-Files*, but that she has true lore of her own in Giles' books where he can look up important "stuff." Later, she references the other half of the FBI paranormal-exploration duo when she turns invisible and explains that Xander and Anya are working on reversing the process. She says they are "Mulder-ing out what happened" ("Gone" 6.11). *Supernatural* has several references to *The X-Files*. Eight episodes textually reference *The X-Files*, and seven more offer homages to the show through story-lines, episode titles or other subtle similarities. Aside from simply mentioning *The X-Files* in the dialogue, *Supernatural* takes its pop culture lore one step further than *Buffy* by directly referencing the actors on the show. In "Wishful Thinking" (4.8), Dean describes a possible creature they're chasing as possibly being "a Bigfoot. You know, and he's some kind of alcohol-porno addict. Kind of like a deep-woods Duchovny," making a joke about David Duchovny's real-life issues.[1]

Whether making pop culture references or referring to specific urban legends or folklore, all three shows are at least partially responsible for shaping our expectations and cultural understandings of the supernatural, paranormal and just plain weird. But sometimes, the lore that appears on these shows may not be consistent with actual folklore. In *American Folklore* and *Folklore and Fakelore*, Richard Dorson explains this concept as being what he calls "fakelore." For Dorson and others, fakelore is the antithesis of folklore, "popular culture bowdlerizations rather than authentic products of the folk imagination. … [fakelore] is the intentional invention of "folky"-like "lore," often for commercial or advertising purposes. It might look like folklore and sound like folklore, but it is inauthentic" (Koven and Thorgeirsdottir 188). Koven and Thorgeirsdottir have another explanation, however, that

---

[1] *Supernatural* also exists in a universe where *Buffy* is a television show. In "Hell House" (1.17), two side characters try to psych themselves up for entering a haunted house and ask each other "What would Buffy do?"

allows all three shows to take whatever liberties are deemed necessary for the lore and the

plotlines to work together while still considering what they offer to be folklore instead of

fakelore. Instead of saying that the lore used by shows such as *Supernatural* is fakelore,

Koven and Thorgeirsdottir posit the concept of "television folklore" (190), based off of critic

Juwen Zhang's "filmic folklore."

Filmic folklore is defined as "an imagined folklore that exists only in films, and is a

folklore or folklore-like performance that is represented, created, or hybridized in fictional

film" (Zhang 267). Taking into account how many supernatural television shows have

saturated the entertainment industry, Koven and Thorgeirsdottir argue that something similar

could exist on television as "television folklore." Television folklore is an imagined folklore

that exists only in television shows, that is a hybrid of traditional folklore, pop culture

interpretations – such as when *Buffy* or *Supernatural* make onscreen references to other

popular supernatural shows – and lore created specifically for their own storylines. These

shows are not trying to invent a new folklore or challenge the existing lore, as Dorson's

fakelore theory would suggest. Instead, they are intentionally making connections that are

fully recognizable as true folklore and pop culture inventions at the same time (Koven and

Thorgeirsdottir 187). So when we watch an episode of *Buffy* or *Supernatural*, we understand

that we are not getting one-hundred percent true folklore, but we know enough of it to

understand why and how it has been changed.

I would argue that a similar phenomenon has developed over the last twenty years

that creates a sort of filmic/television religion. This television religion builds off of existing

religious beliefs and tweaks them as necessary, often calling attention to those changes

specifically, such as when Bobby talks about the prophecy of Revelation in the bible. He says

that the bible is a "widely distributed version" of the truth that is "just for tourists" ("Are You
There God? It's Me, Dean Winchester" 4.2). Just like when characters from *Buffy* or
Supernatural acknowledge *The X-Files* as an existent television show in their universes,
Bobby mentions the official/traditional lore of the bible and then sets up how his research is
the "reality." The changes or interpretations to religion on television are not meant as a way
to sway religious belief among the viewers or even as a direct representation of how that
belief has already been changed; however, there is some value in looking at how often
television religion mimics shifts in real-world patterns of belief. The question then becomes
this: how do we examine this mimicry and shift – through strict literary criticism or applying
a different methodology?

Examining television religion requires a combination of literary criticism and what
Harold Bloom calls religious criticism in *The American Religion*: "a mode of description,
analysis, and judgment that seeks to bring us closer to the workings of the religious
imagination" (3). For Bloom, literary criticism relies upon aesthetic dimensions within texts,
while religious criticism focuses on the spiritual aspects of religious texts and phenomena
(3).[2] This focus on the spiritual is why I argue that a discussion of television religion requires
a combination of the two types of criticism. Applying religious criticism to shows that are
created by non-religious writers or that are not meant to have a direct religious impact, would
mean looking at only half the work. It is also somewhat difficult to accomplish, as "any
movement from another kind of criticism to religious criticism invokes the shadows of
revisionism, a movement of the mind that causes every one of us to ask … how can I open

---

[2] This view of literary criticism relying mainly upon aesthetic dimensions is somewhat dated, and arguments
can be made that branches – like cultural criticism – do not fit this definition. I have chosen to use it, however,
for two reasons. First, it is one of the few discussions that put literary and religious criticism side-by-side.
Secondly, as I am dealing mainly with visual texts, the discussion of aesthetics seemed fitting.

the traditions of religion to my own experience?" (Bloom, *Post-Christian Nation* 256-257).

The aesthetic focus of literary criticism could help to balance out the spiritual focus of

religious criticism when looking at television religion.

Some critics look at religious criticism as a subset of literary criticism as opposed to a

strictly spiritual discussion, but this movement is still fairly small despite the presence of

academic journals such as *Religion and the Arts, Religion and Literature, Christianity and

Literature, Literature and Theology,* or *Renascence.*[3] Part of the issue is deciding on what

religion is within a textual context – is it real-world religion imagined and interpreted by a

text, or is it an imagined religion based on real-world religion but in possession of its own

dogma?

I believe an acknowledgement of something like a television religion, or even more

broadly, a textual religion, would help open the door for further religious criticism. By

looking at a work critically in regard to its textual religion, we can then establish

comparisons to patterns of real-world belief. Such a discussion would not only provide new

insight into existent works, but also show new cultural relevance for those works. Most of all,

using religious criticism to examine textual religion would allow us to see the impact pop

culture has on deeply-held belief systems and vice-versa.

Throughout this dissertation, I have focused specifically on how *The X-Files, Buffy*

and *Supernatural* have explored Christian mythology and displayed the altered Christ figure,

or Common Christ, within their stories. All three series display their own versions of

religious belief – some blatant, some subtle – that creates a contextual Christianity. Were I

simply to judge or comment on the direct Christian relevance of each, their deviations and

---

[3] For a more in-depth discussion of the state of religious literary criticism, please see Dennis Taylor's article, "The Need for a Religious Literary Criticism."

alterations would be seen as a negative trait. However, accepting that their versions of textual

Christianity are meant to exist within the shows' canon and not as direct reflections of real-

world religion, opens up the possibility of looking at what those differences represent.

So, What's the Point?

In *The Mythic Image*, Joseph Campbell discusses James George Frazer's definition of

religion from *The Golden Bough: A Study of Magic and Religion*. Frazer says that religion is

made up of two elements, "theoretical: a belief in powers higher than man" and "practical: an

attempt to propitiate and please them [the powers]" (qtd in Campbell 430). Campbell adds

his own element to Frazer's religious duo, claiming that there must also exist a mystic or

poet, someone who thinks "neither of God nor of man as an ultimate term, but simply [is] in

awe of the marvel of being and absorbed in the difficult task of self-transformation" (431).

These beings are "achieved in experience, and not merely in belief" and are engaged in "the

willing sacrifice of oneself for the good of another human being" (431). This third element is

where my idea of Common Christs exists. Common Christs are versed in the experiences of

the world. They do not do what they do in order to please the higher powers of the universe –

in most cases they actively go against that sense of authority – but rather to save mankind.

They are trying to find their place in the world and, at the moment, that place has been

determined as a willing sacrifice for humanity. The Common Christs of *The X-Files*, *Buffy*

and *Supernatural* are not out to fulfill some great, religious prophecy. More often than not,

they are usually trying to prevent prophetic fulfillment. They challenge the ruling authority

even as they satisfy the call of sacrifice because they see sacrifice as not being done in the

name of God or religion, but in the service of humanity against fate and forces beyond their

ken.

Religion, traditionally, is hide-bound, wrapped in dogma and text. Looking at religion as it plays out in characters and storylines on television is where we are allowed to explore our beliefs; it is where we see how our changing expectations affect our interpretation and view of religious dogma. There is a split, however, between the idea of religion and belief that is promised by the organized church and the idea of faith and belief that's present in American culture. This split has only continued over time into current expressions of pop culture. To some extent, this discrepancy is responsible for the creation of textual religion within modern literature, film and genre fiction. Shows like *The X-Files, Buffy,* and *Supernatural* are heavily laden with Christian symbolism and iconography, but their representation of organized religion is often that of a corrupt, overpowering body trying to deny or hide "the truth" of personal faith and belief, and in all three series there is a distinct lack of a traditional Christ figure who redeems the characters.

It may not be that Christ has disappeared as a figure from Christian allegory, but that he has evolved from an ethereal being into a common, every-day person like us. Where the Christ of old was described as an enigma by St. Augustine or something viewed as "through a glass, darkly" by St. Paul, the new, American Christ is a friend who "walks with me and talks with me" (Erickson 112). A new creature for a new culture, the modern American Christ is merely a "20th century American whose principal difference is that he has already risen from the dead" (Bloom, *Post-Christian Nation* 65). In the place of traditional Christ figures, we have Common Christs – figures that may bring salvation or redemption, but rarely both; figures who are far from perfect and all too human; figures who know they will have to save the world again and again – their work is never done. The Common Christs of *Buffy* and *Supernatural*, in particular, illuminate this shift away from the one-and-done savior aspect of Christ into the salvation made possible through the acts of the common man that reflects America's uncomfortableness with being saved by a perfect savior.

This evolution of the Christ figure into a Common Christ, one who takes salvation from a perfect being and places it into the hands of an imperfect common man, represents a shift not only in how we receive these characters but also in how we produce and respond to their stories. The creators of both *Buffy* and *Supernatural* have expressed their desire to create heroes and saviors out of the common man as opposed to having an all-powerful being come down and save us. Joss Whedon, creator and writer of *Buffy* claims, "We don't need heroes so much as recognizing ourselves as heroes." And *Supernatural* creator and writer Eric Kripke declares that, "Salvation has to lie with your main characters, or else what's the point?" As American Christianity continues to evolve and more and more people leave traditional churches for non-denominational ones, it will be interesting to see if this trend of viewing ourselves as heroes responsible for our own salvation continues to appear in the lives of our fictional saviors.